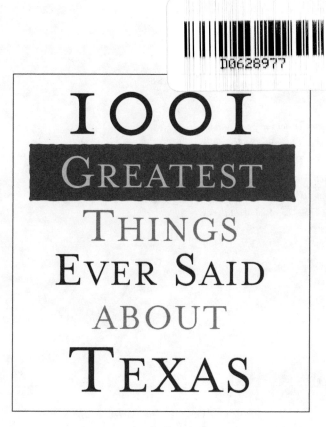

1001
GREATEST
THINGS
EVER SAID
ABOUT
TEXAS

ALSO FROM THE LYONS PRESS

1001

GREATEST

THINGS
EVER SAID
ABOUT
TEXAS

Edited and with an Introduction by

Donna Ingham

THE LYONS PRESS
Guilford, Connecticut
An imprint of The Globe Pequot Press

The Lyons Press is an imprint of The Globe Pequot Press.

10 9 8 7 6 5 4 3 2 1

Printed in the United States of America

Designed by Carol Sawyer/Rose Design

ISBN 13: 978-1-59228-998-1

ISBN 10: 1-59228-998-3

Library of Congress Cataloging-in-Publication Data is available on file.

CONTENTS

Texas—it's like a whole other country.

—*Texas Department of Economic
Development slogan*

INTRODUCTION

I'm ruined for reading, and for much of any other kind of communication, for that matter. I think I'll never again be able to pick up a book, magazine, or newspaper or listen to a newscast or watch a movie or television program without looking for or listening for a good quotation about Texas.

And there are lots of them out there. From the time folks first started arriving in Texas, they were talking about it—about its size and its varied landscape and its people. They recorded their thoughts about frontier hardships and opportunities, about battles and independence and statehood, about food and sports and other events, and about each other.

Moreover, people who have never lived in Texas talk about it as well. It has its own mystique created in part by its unique history— the only state to have fought its own revolution to become an independent country, after all—and in part by Hollywood versions of the

Old West. Visitors come with their own expectations, sometimes met and sometimes not. They are likely to leave with the notion that Texas is, as John Steinbeck says, "a state of mind," a concept, an idea that will always be part myth and part reality.

There is little middle ground, apparently, when it comes to people's opinions about Texas and Texans. They're likely to either wax rhapsodic about the place and the people or offer up the most vitriolic kind of condemnation.

All that makes for interesting reading, especially when one juxtaposes the one against the other. For example, it's one thing for an icon of Texas history like Sam Houston to say "Texas is the finest portion of the globe that has ever blessed my vision," and quite another for Yankee Civil War general Philip Henry Sheridan to say "If I owned Hell and Texas, I would rent out Texas and live in Hell."

Certain aspects of the Lone Star State seem to be the most attention-grabbing. The boasting about the size and quality of all things Texan, for example, leads Edward Smith to claim "Texans ignore 'better,' long ago forgot the useless word 'good.' Everything in Texas is 'best.'" The state's weather vagaries have prompted sayings such as "Nobody but fools and newcomers predict the weather in Texas," and Peg Hein observes that "When Texans were asked to list the ten things they liked best about Texas and the ten things they liked least, weather headed both lists."

Texas has its cowboys, its oil men, its outlaws, its Texas Rangers—both the law enforcement officers and the baseball team— and, nowadays, its astronauts and its millionaire businessmen and businesswomen. It claims to have America's Team, the Dallas Cow-boys, and counts three U. S. presidents from within its borders (four, if you include Dwight D. Eisenhower, born in Texas before his family defected back to Kansas). All of these, and more, have inspired memorable lines from Texans and non-Texans alike.

Some categories deserve and get their own sections in this collection. Politics, certainly, is fertile ground for commentary. And, as columnist Molly Ivins says, politics in Texas is the "finest form of free entertainment ever invented." The politicians themselves have found colorful ways to describe the state of their status and their state and the union. Texan John Nance (Cactus Jack) Garner, vice presi-dent under Franklin Roosevelt, summed up his office as one that "didn't amount to a hill of beans," and, even more graphically, as one that "isn't worth a pitcher of warm spit." From former governor Joseph Sayers we have "A Texas governor has only two happy days: the day he is inaugurated and the day he retires." When George W. Bush was governor, he announced, "I have set high standards for our public schools, and I have met those standards." That's good.

Sports, too, capture the imaginations and test the verbal skills in Texas. In particular, there is football. "Football is to Texans what religion is to a priest." So said legendary Dallas Cowboys coach Tom Landry. In spite of the fact that rodeo is the official state sport, foot-ball dominates the sports sections in Texas newspapers and brings forth some memorable lines from both fans and players. Rosemary Kent says, "Some people believe the main reason there is a public school system is to give Texans more football teams to root for." Beyond football, Texas has other sports and sports heroes too, of course. When he won his first major golf tournament, it was Lee Trevino who said, "I'm so happy, I'm gonna buy the Alamo and give it back to Mexico." And champion race driver A. J. Foyt admits, "I feel safer on a race track than I do on Houston's freeways." Seven-time Tour de France winner Lance Armstrong says, "A bicycle is the long-sought means of transportation for all of us who have run-away hearts."

In the arts, Texas claims unique music: cowboy songs "rhythmed to the walk, the trot and the gallop of horses," as J. Frank Dobie says, and honkytonk, that Paul Crume says turned into rock-and-roll, "with the same squirmy rhythm, the same baying-at-the-moon style of singing." Texas has its poets and writers who "must live with two gigantic images: the fantasy world of cowboys, Indians, and rich oil-men and the real world of hardship, subsistence, and stagnation," according to Lera Patrick Tyler Lich.

Texas speech, in and of itself, is full of quotable words and phrases. From the Texans' favorite verb, "fixin' to," to nouns like "dogie" ("a calf whose mammy has died and whose pappy has run off with another cow"—Boyce House) and "maverick" ("a person who makes his own rules, someone who marches to his own beat"—Peg Hein), one could make a sizeable glossary. So those and others show up in the section on lingo, sayings, and superstitions.

Compiling these 1001 entries has taken me to books, magazines, newspapers, billboards and road signs, radio, television, Web sites, and individuals who might remember old songs or sayings or supersti-tions. This compilation is by no means complete and could never be.

It represents simply the best I could find in the time I had allotted. The final section is not so much quotations about Texas as it is quotations by famous Texans, but some are just too good to leave out: Ma Ferguson's "If English was good enough for Jesus Christ, it's good enough for me"; Clint Murchison, Sr.'s "Money is like manure. Pile it all in one place and it stinks like hell. Spread it around and it does a lot of good"; Lady Bird Johnson's "Every politician should have been born an orphan and remain a bachelor."

If some topics seem particularly loaded—the Alamo, Texas Rangers, football, politics—that is at least partially because those are areas that seem to fire the imaginations of Texans.

That said, I can already see gaps I'd like to fill in if we could continue this project forever. We can't. But I'll keep looking for the words well said, insightfully recorded, and Texas focused. And that's a fact.

DONNA INGHAM
SPICEWOOD, TEXAS
JULY 2006

A STATE OF MIND

OF MIND

Texas, the Place

Texas is a state of mind. Texas is an obsession. Above all, Texas is a nation in every sense of the word. And there's an opening convey of generalities. A Texan outside of Texas is a foreigner.

—*John Steinbeck*

Texas mystique [has been] created by the chemistry of the frontier in the crucible of history and forged into an enduring state of heart and mind.

—*T. R. Fehrenbach*

There is a special mystique to Texas. Texans represent many things to the uninitiated: We are bigger than life in our boots and Stetsons, rugged individualists whose two-steppin' has achieved world-wide acclaim, and we were the first to define hospitality.

—*Ann Richards*

[T]he idea of Texas remains a compelling part of the state's imaginative power. It is the spirit of the place—warts and all—that continues long after the deaths of Crockett, Bowie, Audie Murphy, and Lyndon Johnson.

—*Mark Busby*

Texas is my mind's country, that place I most want to understand and record and preserve. Four generations of my people sleep in its soil; I have children there, and a grandson; the dead past and the living future tie me to it.

—*Larry L. King*

Texas one and indivisible

—*motto on Texas state seal*

Texas is a blend of valor and swagger.

—*Carl Sandburg*

Texas, the gathering place of the most restless and imaginative spirits in the union, inclines naturally to the romantic.

—*Jane McManus Cazneau*

Perhaps [Texas] is, at least I hope it is, still a little old-fashioned in the high emphasis it has always placed on personal friendships, on the camaraderie of casual cohorts working together on a ranch, an oil rig or whatever.

—*George Sessions Perry*

Almost everything about Texas reveals some trademark of an
iron will.

—*AAA Texas Tour Book, 2005*

Other states were carved or born; Texas grew from hide and horn.
—*Berta Hart Nance*

I began to understand that all Texas is an eternal synthesis of past
and present, superimposed one upon the other. It produces a feeling
of being in two places at once.

—*Mary Lasswell*

I must say as to what I have seen of Texas, it is the garden spot of the world, the best land and the best prospects for health I ever saw, and I do believe it is a fortune to any man to come here. There is a world of country here to settle.

—*David Crockett*

Texas is the finest portion of the globe that has ever blessed my vision.

—*Sam Houston*

Texas is strong country. It's optimistic country with blue skies, white fleecy clouds, warm sunshine.

—*Liz Carpenter*

Texas is a great state. It's the "Old Man River" of states. No matter who runs it or what happens to it politically, it just keeps rolling along.

—*Will Rogers*

I've traveled all over the world, but I don't think there is any place better than Texas.

—*Red Adair*

I couldn't believe Texas was real. When I arrived there, there wasn't a blade of green grass or a leaf to be seen, but I was absolutely crazy about it. There wasn't a tree six inches in diameter at that time. For me Texas is the same big wonderful thing that the oceans and the highest mountains are.

—*Georgia O'Keeffe*

I done drew the line. Just like the Alamo. You're either on one side of the line or the other. I don't want to ever leave Texas again.

—*Bum Phillips*

You will never have the pleasure of hearing how loud a whip can be cracked until you come to Texas.

—*Alfred Howell*

Texas is OK if you want to settle down and do your own thing quietly, but it's not for outrageous people, and I was always outrageous.

—*Janis Joplin*

If Texas were a sane place, it wouldn't be nearly as much fun.

—*Molly Ivins*

Texas is worse than any other state because she has never
been whipped.

—*David Stanley*

If I owned Hell and Texas, I would rent out Texas and live in Hell.

—*Philip Henry Sheridan*

Texas has more trees and less timber; more rivers and less water; more resources and less cash; more itinerant preachers and less religion; more cows and less milk, and you can see farther and see less than any damn country in the world.

—*Ben (Pitchfork) Tillman*

Within my knowledge, there is not a country of the same extent that has more poor land; that has a greater number of local causes of disease—that has more unseemly and disagreeable swamps and ponds, or that has more snakes, mosquitoes, ticks and flies than Texas.

—*James W. Parker*

The vermin, the famine, hot winds and dry soil, which caused clouds of dust to fill the sultry air in July and August and lodge on everything, made me begin to think . . . that it would have been better to remain in New Orleans and keep a thread and needles store than go to Texas.

—*Teresa Griffin Vielé*

Calling a taxi in Texas is like calling a rabbi in Iraq.

—*Fran Lebowitz*

Maybe the heat . . . maybe the jalapenos . . . maybe the cowboys . . . something ignited my passion to move to Texas.

—*Rose Potter*

So at first the visitor will view Texas as a land of contrasts. And it is a land of murmuring seacoasts and silent mountains, fertile fields and barren deserts, paved roads and stony trails, skyscrapers and adobe huts.

—*Herbert A. White*

Texas . . . is an inclined plane tilted suggestively toward the Gulf of Mexico which still has in its yawning chasms room for unlimited consignments of soil fertility. In periods of excessive rainfall . . . a dozen bloated rivers spill over the continental shelf. In droughty seasons, sweepings of vast erosions are blown by violent winds clear from the high plains miles out to sea.

—*Roy Bedichek*

Right from the beginning, folks have been moving to Texas—the Spanish, the French, the Mexicans. In search of gold and paradise, they found only cows and crabgrass.

—*Rosemary Kent*

Texas is remarkable in the respect that it was approached by settlers from several different directions. One result of this condition is reflected in the heterogeneity of the Indian tribes encountered by early travelers in Texas.

—Epic-Century *magazine*

~

The state of Texas is fortunate in possessing a rich and varied folk-lore. When white settlers from the Old South came in bringing their slaves, they found the Mexicans in possession, and before them there were the Indians. These four racial groups maintained their several identities, and, except for the white plantation owner and his hands, they also had different languages, religions, and cultures. Hence their folkways and folklore were distinct and characteristic.

—*Mody C. Boatright, Wilson M. Hudson,*
and Allen Maxwell

~

The bounty of Texas consists of a state full of rich living and traditions, stretching centuries back to the Indians, through the Spanish, Mexicans, and Anglos, to all the many nationalities that moved in, and then spread out through Texas and the Southwest.

—*Frances Edward Abernathy*

Diversity is part of what has made Texas unique. Few countries in the world have been populated with as many diverse cultures. From all over the world came groups looking for a place where they could express their individuality.

—*Jim Gramon*

The thing about Texas is, it's where all of these cultures—Anglo, Tejano, and American Indian cultures—meet.

—*Thomas Knowles*

At age eighty, I have witnessed a lot of Texas history, known a lot
of its heroes and some of its scoundrels, and like many daughters and
great-great-granddaughters of pioneer Texans, thrilled to the great
variety that is Texas.

—Liz Carpenter

I am forced to conclude that God made Texas on his day off, for pure
entertainment, just to prove that all that diversity could be crammed
into one section of earth by a really top hand.

—Mary Lasswell

I have moved over a great part of Texas and I know that within its
borders I have seen just about as many kinds of country, contour,
climate, and conformation as there are in the world.

—John Steinbeck

Within this giant state, the diversity is astounding. The deserts of west Texas, the plains of the north, the semi-arid farmland of south Texas, the rich Blacklands region of central Texas, the Coastal Plains bordering the Gulf of Mexico, and then there are the beautiful Piney Woods and Big Thicket of East Texas.

—*Jim Gramon*

Your Texas is no different than my Texas.

—*Pat Mora*

For all its enormous range of space, climate, and physical appearance, and for all the internal squabbles, contentions, and strivings, Texas has a tight cohesiveness perhaps stronger than any other section of America. Rich, poor, Panhandle, Gulf, city, country, Texas is the obsession, the proper study and the passionate possession of all Texans.

—*John Steinbeck*

Ironically, Texans have historically promoted their state's cultural uniqueness because of its lack of true unity and cohesion.

—*Benjamin Soskis*

Border to border, Texas can boast more quarrelsome characters than any other state.

—*David Carlton*

It is extremely improbable that I shall ever see Texas again, as the first of January, 1899, ushered in my ninety-second year, but I will cherish the memory of the long ago spent on her soil, and wish her a prosperous future. I am proud to note the progress she has made, though I can scarcely realize the transformation that progress has wrought.

—*Noah Smithwick*

I dearly love Texas, but I consider it a harmless perversion on my part, and discuss it only with consenting adults.

—Molly Ivins

Texas will again lift its head and stand among the nations. It ought to do so, for no country upon the globe can compare with its natural advantages.

—Sam Houston

Since you have chosen to elect a man with a timber toe to succeed me, you may all go to hell and I will go to Texas.

—David Crockett

I was, for some years, a member of Congress. In my last canvass, I told the people of my District, that, if they saw fit to re-elect me, I would serve them as faithfully as I had done, but, if not, *they might go to hell and I would go to Texas.* I was beaten, gentlemen, and here I am.

—*David Crockett*

~

Texas—it's like a whole other country.

—*Texas Department of Economic Development slogan*

~

There is a growing feeling that perhaps Texas is really another country, a place where the skies, the disasters, the diamonds, the politicians, the women, the fortunes, the football players and the murders are all bigger than anywhere else.

—*Pete Hamill*

~

I thought I knew Texas pretty well, but I had no notion of its size until I campaigned it.

—*Ann Richards*

In the covered wagon days, if a baby was born in Texarkana while the family was crossing the Lone Star State, by the time they reached El Paso, the baby would be in the third grade.

—*Wallace O. Chariton*

The state of Texas, after having voluntarily sloughed off a lot of surplus square miles in order to round out a few other states, is more than four times the size of all New England, with New York thrown in for *pilón*, and it has a couple of counties that can easily take care of such states as Rhode Island, Delaware, and even Connecticut.

—*Jack C. Butterfield*

You must remember that space is large; it is even larger than Texas.

—*Dr. Werner von Braun*

What you northerners never appreciate . . . is that Texas is so big that you can live your life within its limits and never give a damn about what anyone in Boston or San Francisco thinks.

—*James Michener*

I was always proud of being from Texas and, you know, maybe that was part of fearlessness. I love the fact that Texas is so big, but you don't feel small because of that.

—*Sissy Spacek*

I like the image Texas brings to mind—that of bigness, of strength, of goodness.

—*Ninfa Laurenzo*

Texas is the crossroads of the world. Everything here is big.

—*Bobby Lee*

Farms are so big in Texas that on one of them a man starts out in the Spring and plows a straight furrow right on through until Fall and then he harvests back.

—*Boyce House*

Texas is big now, but imagine the size of her as a republic. Back then the Panhandle had a panhandle.

—*Mike Blakely*

Most Americans can cover their home state in less than a week. In Texas, if you concentrate and work at it steadily, you can traverse your territory by about age thirty-seven.

—*Rosemary Kent*

The Lone Star is a classic symbol in that it conveys both the state's history and its geographic identity in an abstract form: the star signifies brilliance, isolation, distance, and many other things as an abstract form; through the process of association, these become the qualities we associate with Texas the place.

—*Richard V. Francaviglia*

Texas is heaven for men and dogs and hell for women and oxen.
> —*pioneer woman commenting on pioneer conditions*
> *(WPA Guide to Texas); also attributed to Noah*
> *Smithwick and an early German settler in Texas*

After eating, the men might lay down for a little while to rest, but there is no rest for the women. There is always work to be done. In the afternoon there may be more work in the fields, or baking, candlemaking, soap-making, sewing, mending, any of the hundred pressing tasks . . . always something, early and late.
> —*Mathilda Wagner*

Years ago someone pointed out that Texas is hell on women and horses [*sic*]. He was wrong about horses, for most horses are considered to be valuable, and are treated very well.
> —*Larry McMurtry*

Horse trading was one of the cornerstones of life in the Texas west for many years. Your horse was often all that stood between you being successful in life, or being dead. So you had to choose horses carefully, or you'd end up hurtin'.

— *Jim Gramon*

Every wind that drifts the alkali dust from the Goodnight Trail across my home range suggests a land of cattle and horses; every damp breeze carries the penetrating fragrance of greasewood, suggestive of the bold life that rode along it.

— *J. Evetts Haley*

For a few precious moments . . . I'm back in Old Texas, under a high sky, where all things are again possible and the wind blows free.

— *Larry L. King*

Preservation of things American in the Union of our fathers is today's challenge to Texas, above all other states of the American galaxy. Because, in our opinion, the Lone Star State possesses more of those things which have made America great, more of imagination, more of virility, more of native American genius than perhaps any other section of the country.

—*The Pathfinder* (1945)

Maybe it is that Texas is still a pioneer state. No one ever says to anybody in Texas, "Who were your parents?" Your ability to accomplish things is not based on what your family heritage is, as it so often is in the East. It's just based on what *you* can do.

—*Sarah Weddington*

I get from the soil and spirit of Texas the feeling that I, as an individual, can accomplish whatever I want to, and that there are no limits, that you can just keep going, just keep soaring. I like that spirit.

—*Barbara Jordan*

Texas is still a last frontier. It's the part of the United States where the traditional virtues are still operating. In short, a piece of living history.

—*John C. B. Richmond*

. . . Texas's frontier history and geography produce deep feelings of ambivalence. On one hand, the vastness of its area seems to negate borders; on the other, the state's location on the edge of Southern and Western culture and along the long Rio Grande border with Mexico reinforces an awareness of borders.

—*Mark Busby*

If frontier life has left any cultural residue at all, it is a residue of a most unfortunate sort—i.e., that tendency to romanticize violence which is evident on the front page of almost every Texas newspaper almost every day.

—*Larry McMurtry*

Texas humor has not yet left the frontier. It is still rough and ribald, not far removed from a scorpion placed in an unsuspecting boot or a cocklebur under a saddle blanket. It is still designed to shock.

—*Cactus Pryor*

They say that Virginia is the mother of Texas. We never knew who the father was, but we kinda suspected Tennessee.

—*Tex Ritter*

Texas is neither southern nor western. Texas is Texas.

—*William Blakley*

Decades before Horace Greeley gave his famous piece of advice to young men, Texas was considered West. Its temper is still Western, but it is no more Far West than it is Old South. On the map it might logically be classed as Middle West, but in no other way is it so.

—*J. Frank Dobie*

If you've ever driven across Texas, you know how different one area of the state can be from another. Take El Paso. It looks as much like Dallas as I look like Jack Nicklaus.

—*Lee Trevino*

My young friend, when you see anything of that kind [a knife fight] going on in El Paso, don't interfere. It is not considered good manners here.

—*Ben Dowell*

Sarah and I live on the east side of the mountain [near El Paso]. It is the sunrise side, not the sunset side. It is the side to see the day coming, not the side to see the day that has gone. The best day is coming. . . .

—*Tom Lea*

Since I have lived in El Paso, I have developed a need for space that I never had before. I live in a desert, and when I find myself in a forest or a large city, I feel closed in. I need to see the horizon.

—*Diana Natalicio*

[Dallas] is like its women: It has no intention of growing old. The moment an inkling of a wrinkle shows up, it signs on for a lift.

—Helen Bryant Anders

Whether your destination is heaven or hell, you always have to change planes in Dallas.

—Richard (Kinky) Friedman

Go to Dallas for Education, Come to Fort Worth for Entertainment.

—advertisement for Fort Worth's Frontier Centennial Exposition, 1936

That man [Amon Carter] wants the whole government of the
United States to be run for the exclusive benefit of Fort Worth,
and if possible, for the detriment of Dallas.

—*John Nance Garner*

Basically the cleavage between the two cities is of the simplest:
Dallas is where the east ends, and Fort Worth is notoriously "where
the west begins." Dallas is a baby Manhattan; Fort Worth is a cattle
annex. Dallas has the suave and glittering clothes of Neiman Marcus;
Fort Worth has dust and stockyards.

—*John Gunther*

Houston is, without a doubt, the weirdest, most entertaining city in
Texas, consisting as it does of subtropical forest, life in the fast lane,
a layer of oil, cowboys and spacemen.

—*State Travel Guide*, 2004

Is Houston now fun? I vote yes.

True, downtown is still far from the street scene that the city—
and its visitors—would like. And Mapquest's recent proclamation
that it's the hardest city in the nation to navigate is right on. The city
doesn't help matters when it names its neighborhoods: Midtown is
south of downtown, and Uptown is off to the west.

Then there's the heat. And the humidity.

—Helen Bryant Anders

But this city of Houston, this State of Texas, this country of the
United States was not built by those who waited and rested and
wished to look behind them. This country was conquered by those
who moved forward—and so will space.

—John F. Kennedy

[Houston] was a strange city for someone newly arrived from Midland, but a comfortable one once the [George] Bushes realized that there was at least one place in Texas that had the same societal boundaries, circles, and layers as the Northeast. Midland had been, almost, a simple way station where one could make instant friends and instant money.

—*Bill Minutaglio*

[Houston's] children might be interesting to know. They will be natural urbanites, most of them, members of the first generation of Texans to belong in fact and in spirit to a fertile city, not to the Old Man of the country or the Old Maid of the towns.

—*Larry McMurtry*

[Houston] is the ambitious rival of Galveston, and because nature has endowed its streets with unusual capacity for muddiness, Galveston calls its inhabitants "mud-turtles." A free exchange of satiric compliments between the two infant cities is of frequent occurrence.

—Edward King

Give me a miserable, dark, and cold day to visit Galveston. That's when I like to poke along the beach where the sun worshipers frolic in summer. Everything is different in winter. Even the sea gulls behave differently. They sit around on the sea wall in quiet, ruffled groups and remind me of a bunch of old cows, waiting by the fence for somebody to come feed them.

—Leon Hale

To this island [Galveston] we gave the name of Malohado (bad fortune). The people there are large and well-formed. They have no weapons but bows and arrows, in the use of which they are very good.

—Cabeza de Vaca, shipwrecked on Galveston Island in 1528

. . . Austin, Texas, welcomed spring's anticipation—like an aging adolescent who clings to his music long after the days of high school are gone.

—Jodi Thomas

August in Austin is characterized traditionally by the three "H's": hazy, hot, and humid.

—Betsy Noziak and Tricia Henry

ADVERTISER: Name in order the three best newspapers in Texas. Well, the Galveston *News* runs about second, and the San Antonio *Express* third. Let us hear from you again.

—*William Sydney Porter (O. Henry), while editor of* Rolling Stone *newspaper in Austin*

[San Antonio] is an ancient Spanish city pretending to be American.

—*George Sessions Perry*

[San Antonio] parties on. Just look at the game faces on all those people trudging up and down the River Walk. Fun will be had. You betcha.

—*Helen Bryant Anders*

Though the Staked Plains overlap the Panhandle, Texas's ultimate flat spot is likely closer to non-Panhandle Lubbock, where nearby towns are named, fittingly, Brownfield, Plainview, and Levelland.

—*Anne Dingus*

Life in Lubbock, Texas, taught me two things: One is that God loves you and you're going to burn in hell. The other is that sex is the most filthy, awful thing on earth and you should save it for someone you love.

—*Butch Hancock*

Amarillo is literally full of hogs, and the flea crop is very promising—getting ready for the summer visitors. Get another press convention and protracted meeting and invalids coming in needn't bring any flesh brush or other irritants. Amarillo will throw in the fleas with the board and lodging. Come along.

—*Amarillo* News, 1895

Streets were being paved in the residential area [of Amarillo]. More stores—attractive stores—were opening on Polk Street. There were new faces in town every day. The community was charged with a low-key expectancy because of the oil drilling crews in the Canadian River breaks.

—Thomas Thompson

Odessa was the hardscrabble, hard-drinking, honky-tonk underbelly of West Texas. And it was wet, which was what people said about a place in Texas where you could buy a drink and bend the edges on that emptiness.

—Bill Minutaglio

If I were a psychoanalyzer, I might conclude that I was trying to, not compete with my father, but do something on my own. My stay in Texas was no Horatio Alger thing, but moving from New Haven to Odessa just about the day I graduated was quite a shift in lifestyle.

—*George H. W. Bush*

Now there were three things to do in the desert, where tumbleweeds literally tumbled and the spiky bundles pressed against the front doors and the windows, scratching on the screens, latching onto the underneath of your car: *You raised hell in Odessa . . . you raised your family in Midland . . . and you drilled for that deep money.*

—*Bill Minutaglio*

Midland was the ugliest place on the face of the earth. The only reason to be there was because they had oil under the ground.

—*Randall Roden*

When Beaumont was an oil boom town at the turn of the century, its water supply was so bad that doctors urged the influx of new residents to drink whiskey instead.

—*Jack Maguire*

I grew up just at the time when rural and soil traditions in Texas were really, for the first time, being seriously challenged by urban tradition.

—*Larry McMurtry*

Texas can never really be urban, for our urban centers are suffused with rural myths.

—*Craig Clifford*

The hold of the countryside on the Texas mind has more to do with roots than boots. It survives due to the persistence of the notion that the country way of life is better than the city way of life—and that something has been irretrievably lost in the process of urbanization.

—Paul Burka

Highway 8 up in Bowie County will carry you to or take you away from half a dozen tiny farm towns in the northeast corner of Texas. Over the last quarter century or so, it's mostly been carrying people away. The answer to the old question "How you gonna keep 'em down on the farm?" would seem to be—you don't.

—Bob Phillips

Many Texas towns are too small to support one lawyer, but none are too small to support two lawyers.

—Lyndon Baines Johnson

[In 1964] in the small Texas Hill Country town of Johnson City, President [Lyndon] Johnson delivered the commencement address at the school from which he had graduated in 1924. He was in the bosom of rural Texas and Old Democrat country. He talked about the future, one in which "every child will grow up knowing that success in life depends on ability and not on the color of skin or the circumstance of birth."

—*Bill Minutaglio*

Like most little Texas towns, Rockdale is a cheap place to live, a hard place to earn much money.

—*George Sessions Perry*

About ten the next morning I stepped off the ties into a village
that calls itself Atascosa City. I bought a thirty-cent breakfast and
a ten-cent cigar and stood on Main Street jingling the last three
pennies in my pocket—dead broke. A man in Texas with only three
cents in his pocket is no better off than a man who has no money
and owes two cents.

—*William Sydney Porter (O. Henry)*

Texline has been decided upon as the end of the passenger and
freight division on this railroad, and will be built up by the combined
effort of the railroad and the XIT interests, and there is a prevalent
opinion that, as it is right at the line of Texas and New Mexico, close
to No Man's Land and not far from the line of Texas and Colorado, it
will be the biggest and the best and the fastest and the hardest and
the busiest and the wildest and the roughest and the toughest town
of this section.

—*Tascosa* Pioneer, 1888

It doesn't take much to imagine outlaws and lawmen facing off
in front of the old hotel in downtown Lajitas. It's the kind of place
that looks like it never got a face-lift after the Wild West wasn't
wild anymore.

—*Bob Phillips*

Two separate societies, male and female, operated in rural towns
like Archer City. Cut off from frontier experience, men sought new
sources of masculine identity while retaining the traditional Western
discomfort with female society.

—*Lera Patrick Tyler Lich*

No B. B. King or Beale Street here, but this Texas Panhandle community [Memphis] projects its own kind of harmony between two forks
of the Red River.

—*Peggy Heinkel-Wolfe*

Every Texan has a favorite small town. I would be hard-pressed to choose among Hunt, near Kerrville, where the forks of the Guadalupe join and I spent three summers as a camper and a counselor; Hallettsville, halfway between Houston and San Antonio on a forgotten highway, with its grand courthouse and square; and Fort Davis, which still manages to be quaint in the face of creeping chicness.

—*Paul Burka*

It [the town of Blanco] was idyllic, because the river ran through there, and the country was full of wildlife. I lived on a ranch. Most of my friends lived on ranches. On occasion, friends and I would sneak out at night and go hunting with our dogs. Fences didn't mean much, and we'd go for miles. We'd sell the hides to earn a little spending money. It was a boy's world. It was just wonderful.

—*William Wittliff*

Between the railroad and the houses, nearly a mile distant, stretched the Velasco prairie. This prairie was to have as much effect on my childhood imagination as the [Brazos] River and the Gulf [of Mexico].

—*Bertha McKee Dobie*

Electra was a raw, frontier community with growing pains and almost no physical attractiveness, but it had good people and civic pride and school loyalty.

—*Llerena Friend*

Fredericksburg is a quaint little German community in the Texas Hill Country that is a perfect combination of its European and Western past. It's lariats and lederhosen, ten gallons and Tiroleans. It's the kind of place you never want to leave.

—*Bob Phillips*

Ah! what do we know of the beyond? We know that death comes, and we return no more to our world of trouble and care—but where do we go? Are there lands where no traveler has been? A chaos— perhaps where no human foot has trod—perhaps Bastrop. . . .

—*William Sydney Porter* (*O. Henry*)

Everybody's somebody in Luckenbach.

—*Hondo Crouch*

The train doesn't stop in Wills Point, Texas, anymore. Like the rushing hands of time, it roars through town, leaving in its wake only distant memories of the way things used to be. The old bank, the soda fountain, a dry goods store.

—*Bob Phillips*

Like many another rural community across the plains and prairies of West Texas, Pyron lives when nearly all visible traces have vanished. That it can still be seen by the discerning eye and felt by the understanding heart is due to such intangibles as community spirit, country cussedness, and the indelible stamp of place upon the human psyche.

—*Jane Gilmore Rushing*

On a dusty road outside Marfa, Texas, where the Chinati Mountains cut a jagged line across the horizon, strange lights illuminate the sky. These are not the stuff of fantastic, back-road abductions. No, the Marfa Lights are one of the most reliable mysteries in the world. They materialize almost every evening, like clockwork. . . .

—*Frank Bures*

The Texas Rangers most likely are the only law enforcement body in the United States—probably the world—to have a city named in their honor. . . . [D]own in Cameron County, in the lower Rio Grande Valley, is a small community called Rangerville. Nowhere in Texas, though, has there ever been a community named Police, Sheriff, FBI, Royal Canadian Mounted Police, or Scotland Yard.

—*Mike Cox*

It is perhaps the "authenticity" . . . that gives this region [Lower Rio Grande Valley] its definite character. Roma, Brownville and Laredo's central town sites, Mier and San Ygnacio are readily perceived as real survivors of another time. . . .

—*Mario L. Sánchez*

If you're from Chillicothe, Texas, sometimes you get the feeling it's not a real place. It's one of those hallucinations folks have. . . . Maybe the reason Chillicothe isn't real is because Chillicothe doesn't have much reason for existence. The only reason it's there is to give folks from Vernon and Quanah something to feel superior about.

—*Robert Flynn*

From Jacksboro I early found the Texas triptych—Texas fact, fiction, and folklore.

—*Joyce Gibson Roach*

The most precious possession I took away [from Velasco] is not easy to state. It was a capacity for rapture in the presence of natural objects and forces, not always, just sometimes.

—*Bertha McKee Dobie*

Here in Jefferson we have eccentric people and we attract
eccentric people.

—*Juanita Wakefield-Chitwood*

As the old joke goes, this beautiful little town [of Cumby] is so small
that both city limits signs are on the same post.

—*Jim Gramon*

In Electra there were no trees; Sherman had trees; Sherman's birds
were no respecters of white crepe hats.

—*Llerena Friend*

Salado is located, as the joke goes, "about a quarter of a mile from
Resume Speed."

—*Liz Carpenter*

Another special feature of Sour Lake, that alone is sufficient to make it famous, is the springs that cure women of those diseases that are particular to their sex and nine out of ten women are thus afflicted.

—*prospectus of the Sour Lake Company,* 1896

P. S. Is the soil sandy?
Does the wind blow?
Do you have flees [*sic*]?
Does it snow in winter?

—*Mrs. A. B. Schultz in letter to C. W. Post about Post City,* 1911

Of seven newspapers in the Panhandle each claims its town to be the present and prospective metropolis. As a matter of fact, there are and will be some good towns in the Panhandle, but the rest need only settle among themselves the question of second place, for Tascosa will inevitably rank first. Evidences of the fact accumulate every day.

—*Tascosa* Pioneer, 1887

Hemphill County, CANADIAN, the County Seat. The Eldorado of the West. The Greatest Cattle Shipping Point in the World. Bound to eclipse All Other Cities within 250 miles of Her. The Best City Platted in 25 years. Backed by Millions.

—*Canadian* Free Press, 1887

After the *Amarillo Daily News* crowed that Canadian was about to become a ghost town, its mayor, Malouf "Oofie" Abraham . . . raised funds to install 61 mercury-vapor lamps downtown. "If we're going to be a ghost town, we'll be the best damn lit ghost town in the United States," he reportedly huffed.

—*John Morthland*

Gruene, Texas, is nothing more than the intersection of Gruene and Hunter Streets, just north of New Braunfels. The speed limit is somewhere between slow and easy.

—*Bob Phillips*

I was born close to New Braunfels in 1894. We learned to speak
English as very young children. . . . But it was mostly German that
we spoke in the home or with neighbors. We just had nine grades
and we spoke mostly German on the school grounds. It was a
German community with very few English-only speakers.

—*Lillian Stieler, from* Texans: Oral Histories
from the Lone Star State, *1991*

A place more beautiful than Potter's Point [on Caddo Lake] it would
be impossible to imagine. I never tired of admiring the scenery that
lay about my new home. Our home stood upon a jutting promontory
that rose into a hill set in the midst of one of the grandest timber
belts in Texas.

—*Harriet A. Moore Page Potter Ames*

Not a saloon in Jones County. Do you know that we consider that the grandest thing that could be said in our favor? Not a saloon in Jones County! Does not that one sentence speak volumes in favor of morality and sobriety of our town and country?

—*from* Jones County, Texas: A Monthly Publication for Home-Seekers, *1891*

Settings of any kind are most dramatic when first viewed from the edges. Archer County, Texas, is situated twenty miles south of the Oklahoma border and just west of the ninety-eighth meridian, the "institutional fault line" that, according to Walter Prescott Webb, separates two civilizations of the United States.

—*Lera Patrick Tyler Lich*

Texas is diverse enough that its geography can appeal to all kinds of folks. You like mountains? Got 'em. Beaches? Plenty, and their white sands and temperate waters are pure solace for the soul. Deserts? Yep, look out for tumbleweeds. Plains? Heavens, yes! Oh, and fields of flowers splash blue, yellow and red for miles upon miles upon miles.

—*AAA Texas Tour Book*, 2005

When non-natives think of Texas, they usually imagine cowboys and cattle ranches and wide-open spaces. As Texans, we know that our vast state encompasses many diverse and beautiful landscapes— from the deep green East Texas Piney Woods and the cerulean seascapes of the Coastal Bend, to the rolling Texas Hill Country and the magnificent mountains of Big Bend.

—*Peg Champion*

East Texas, where they do things *right*, not cloddish.

—*Mary Lasswell*

In the Piney Woods of East Texas, Nature lays down a wondrous welcome mat. Carpeted with fragrant pine needles, brimming with lakes both mammoth and mysterious, and seasonally rich with radiant roses, delicate dogwoods, and exquisite azaleas, this inviting area both fascinates and captivates.

—*Texas State Travel Guide, 2004*

In that vast evergreen heaven called East Texas, pine and mixed-hardwood forests reign supreme. Here, the sky cradles a rolling landscape, inlaid with venerable pillars of oak, sweetgum, maple, dogwood, and fragrant pine.

—*Stephen Myers and Janet R. Edwards*

Germany's Black Forest has nothing on East Texas. Fact is, the national forests in Texas are some of the thickest woods anywhere in the world, and the kind you'll see more than any other is the good old southern yellow pine. They're as common as ticks on a ranch dog here. . . .

—*Bob Phillips*

East Texas is a red clay road underneath an umbrella of trees. The roadway is dark because no sun can pass through.

—*Tumbleweed Smith*

During the Civil War the [Big Thicket] area became a refuge for service-dodging Texans, and gangs of bush-whackers, as they were called, hid in its fastnesses.

—*The WPA Guide to Texas*

Don't try it without a guide, but the interior of the Big Thicket offers more beauty and pure adventure per square foot than almost any spot left in America.

—*Jack Maguire*

Many miles from the modern-day hurly-burly and rich in primeval border mystique, the Sabine [River] slips down the Louisiana line past forests and swamps like a giant water snake slithering through an ancestral dream.

—*Charlie Llewellin*

The vast Gulf of Mexico weaves its watery spell upon seafarers and landlubbers alike. In Texas, "land ho!" is as exciting a cry as "anchors aweigh!" For, in addition to the bounty of the shimmering sea surfing its shores, Texas offers an abundance of terrific terra firma along its 624-mile coastline.

—*Texas State Travel Guide, 2004*

The flatness of the Texas Coastal Prairies is sometimes broken by dark woods and marshes and growths of huge old live oaks waving Spanish moss. But as a general thing, and in the eye of a person searching for natural beauty, this prairie is some of the ugliest and dullest real estate in all of Texas.

—*Leon Hale*

The rivers of Texas are practically a religion.

—*Sophia Dembling*

Imagine a two-lane road twisting and turning through a valley of shrub-covered limestone hills. Now visualize sparkling lakes nestled in these valleys, slow-moving rivers, fields of wildflowers, and communities rich in German heritage. Welcome to the Texas Hill Country.

—*Thomas M. and Regina M. Ciesla*

[W]e drifted up to the Hill Country, where the people talk slow, the hills embrace you, and the small towns flash by like bright stations reflecting on the windows of a train at night.

—Richard (Kinky) Friedman

Like a songbird in springtime, you can flit from spot to spot [in the Texas Hill Country] before nesting in a streamside cabin. There, the sweet sounds of birdsong and a burbling creek will wash over you like a forgotten nursery rhyme.

—Elaine Robbins

In the spring, the Texas Hill Country is the cradle for thousands of acres of wildflowers.

—B. L. Priddy

Maybe it's the serene valleys tucked between rolling, cedar-studded hills . . . or the abundant indigo and scarlet wildflowers of spring. Perhaps it's the cypress trees that line meandering riverbanks . . . or the friendly small towns where time ticks at a slower tock. Then, again, it could be the siren song of Austin's musical melting-pot. Whatever the appeal, the Texas Hill Country captivates fans the world over.

—*Texas State Travel Guide*, 2004

If there were ever a Garden of Eden in Texas, [Krause Springs] would be it. Limestone shelves, bluffs, and cypresses form a lush sanctuary along meandering Cypress Creek. A waterfall flanked by tufts of lacy maidenhair fern spills over a bluff that shelters a small cave.

—Texas Journey *magazine, May/June* 2006

Colorado Bend State Park . . . feels as familiar and unpretentious as a George Strait song.

—*Charlie Llewellin*

In Big Bend country, the sky's no limit. Nowhere else in Texas do the stars at night shine quite so bright or the sunsets seem quite so rosy. Here, too, the earth displays its own vigor. Prickly pear cacti bloom with fuchsia ferocity and golden exuberance, as desert vistas shimmer far into the distance. Nomadic tumbleweeds bounce erratically across lonesome prairies, and craggy mountain peaks form a jagged phalanx on the horizon.

—*Texas State Travel Guide, 2004*

There [the Big Bend area] lies in its gorgeous splendor and
geological confusion, almost as if it fell from the hands of its
Creator. It fascinates every observer because it seems to be made
of the scraps left over when the world was made, containing samples
of rivers, deserts, blocks of sunken mountains, and tree-clad peaks,
dried-up lakes, canyons, cuestas, vegas, playas, arroyos, volcanic
refuse, and hot springs.

—*Walter Prescott Webb*

In westernmost Texas the Rio Grande cuts its way between Mount
Franklin and the Juárez mountains, becomes an international boundary, and starts its way to the sea. This is a land of harsh, wild beauty,
of arching skies, abrasive winds, sand and seering sun, of cotton-
woods, cactus, and mesquite.

—*William Weber Johnson*

Texas owns the north bank of the Rio Grande, the only river in the world that is navigable to pedestrians.

—Boyce House

When early cowboys and ranchers got their first good look at the Marfa Plateau—the rich grasslands 4,830 feet above the desert, surrounded by far-off mountains and domed by a vast sky that made them feel both grand and puny at the same time—you'd like to think they were struck gloriously dumb.

—Michael Hall

The silhouette of a gaunt jackrabbit in the scant shade of an ocotillo met my gaze as I ascended the rocky hillside in the vast Chihuahuan Desert region south of Alpine. Lazy monsoon clouds floated like giant battleships in an ocean of blue, teasing the parched desert below with great mobile shadows racing across the landscape.

—Wyman Meinzer

Between San Antonio and the Rio Grande River lies a thorny pocket known as "brush country," a nettlesome assortment of bunch grass, prickly pear and other shrubs.

—AAA Texas Tour Book, 2005

Suggest a cattle drive and our minds reflect pictures of John Wayne types in big hats moving from the Texas Brush Country, or *brasada*, to Kansas railheads.

—Jeff Carroll

It is an empire that claims more brush country than any ranch in Texas. At nearly a million acres, you'd be hard-pressed to find a bigger ranch in the world. They say winter comes to the north side of the King Ranch a full month before it finds its way down to the south forty.

—Bob Phillips

West Texas was, and is, as demanding a social environment as its natural elements are demanding.

—A. C. Greene

It's so dry in West Texas the trees follow the dogs around.

—anonymous

In West Texas you have to dig [mesquite roots] for wood and climb [canyons] for water.

—anonymous

A crow has to carry his own rations when he flies over West Texas.

—*anonymous*

Something about the sunbaked, dry air in West Texas mummifies the body and invigorates the spirit.

—*Paul Crume*

In this land, light descends from above but also rises from the land, *la tierra madre*, reflecting its old bones.

—*Pat Mora*

Out in West Texas, the sky is bigger than other places. There are no hills or trees. The only building is an occasional filling station, and those are scarce. How the westward settlers decided to keep moving in the face of all that nothing, I can't imagine. The scenery is blank, and the sky total.

—*Mary Karr*

It was the sky that was Texas, the sky that welcomed me back. The land I didn't care for all that much—it was bleak and monotonous and full of ugly little towns. The sky was what I had been missing, and seeing it again in its morning brightness made me realize suddenly why I hadn't been myself in many months.

—*Larry McMurtry*

The stars at night are big and bright at the McDonald Observatory which sits high atop Mount Locke in the Davis Mountains.

—*Peg Hein*

West Texas is home to me. It is a place which possesses a unique, two-hearted beauty. From its breathtaking sunsets, to its brilliant starry nights, to its serpentine fields of snow-white cotton, a person cannot help but feel the opportunity here.

—*Marsha Sharp*

Here, in West Texas, it was easy to develop an edge, a blunt tongue, to become, in some ways, like one of the oilmen sharpened by repeated defeats.

—*Bill Minutaglio*

Go to a brush arbor revival some Sunday and listen to the reverence with which [West Texans] sing, "Shall We Gather at the River" or "Roll, Jordan, Roll." It's not heaven for which they long; it's pure fresh sweet water.

—Jane Roberts Wood

The [grain] elevators were the tallest buildings on the plains, symmetrical, their thrusting shapes seeming to entrap kinetic energy.

—Annie Proulx

[I]f you live in West Texas, you'd better deal honestly, because folks can see you coming for miles. It is a land of possibility and infinite skies; consequently, it's a terrific place to have big dreams.

—Marsha Sharp

[W]e find some West Texans are . . . Eastern-prejudiced.

—*Barbara Bush*

[Y]ou cannot go down to Texas wearing brown oxfords. Take my word for it. I've spent enough time down there to know a pair of brown oxfords can set you back with those people.

—*Annie Proulx*

The modern inhabitants of the Llanos [Southern Plains] are descendants of recent pioneers, and their mythological heroes are pioneer heroes—Indian fighters and buffalo hunters, cattle ranchers and sodbusting farmers. These kinds of mythic heroes, unfortunately, are becoming rusty relics in the modern West, with its worries about droughts, poisoned and depleted aquifers, creeping desertification and the Greenhouse Effect, and the shrinkage of wilderness and of biological and cultural diversity.

—*Dan Flores*

The Texas Rolling Plains is a big, beautiful land. Bounded on the south by the Edwards Plateau, the west by the Caprock Escarpment, the Cross Timbers on the east, and the Red River in the north, the red plains cut a broad swath through Texas' midsection.

—*Russell A. Graves*

[E]ven fenced and cut with roads the overwhelming presence of grassland persisted, though nothing of the original prairie remained. It was all flat expanse and wide sky. . . . Irrigated circles of winter wheat, dotted with stocker calves, grew on land as level as a runway.

—*Annie Proulx*

I first saw the Texas Panhandle in 1872, when I was a Texas Ranger. . . .
To say I "saw" the Panhandle then ain't right for I was ridin' nights
hidin' in the daytime. . . . I ain't no hero and don't try to make me out
none. All I knowed about the Panhandle was that it was damn good
country to stay out of.

—*anonymous author, Amarillo*
News-Globe, *Aug. 14, 1938*

We [in the Panhandle] like to call [Route 66] the mother road,
because everybody just kinda fled to the road, hoping the road would
take them to better times and better things in their life.

—*Delbert Trew*

Every [Panhandle] town had a motto: "The Town Where No One
Wears a Frown"; "The Richest Land and the Finest People"; "10,000
Friendly people and One or Two Old Grumps."

—*Annie Proulx*

The Panhandle plains. Some folks call this region of Texas gloriously flat, some say it's just plain glorious. These vast, open lands—like the overwhelming expanses of the ocean—often evoke superlatives and always excite the imagination.

—Texas State Travel Guide, 2004

The much-maligned Panhandle acquired its reputation as a topographical tortilla chiefly because most people see it only from Interstate 40, which bisects it at its most horizontal (i.e. cheapest to pave) section.

—Anne Dingus

I have been affected by growing up in the Texas Panhandle where the land is flat or gently rolling, and there is nothing to obscure the horizon. There is something liberating about being able to see into the distance; we people on the High Plains can become claustrophobic when too many trees or mountains block the view.

—*Pauline Durrett Robertson*

I admit to the richness and the softness and the luxuriance of the Panhandle landscape generally now, but not to a beauty superior to that I knew. For the landscape that moves a man most powerfully is the landscape in his mind, the country that comes back in dreams and unguarded reveries. It grew up in his mind when he wasn't looking.

—*Paul Crume*

The Texas Panhandle today is a great breadbasket and beef factory, with vast fields of wheat, maize and corn, dozens of large cattle feed-lots, thousands of square miles of native grasslands.

—Elmer Kelton

Although the land is rugged, it still has a softness about it. Slight breezes make the junipers sway in rhythmic syncopation with the wind. Mornings bring crimson rays of sunlight spilling across the mesquite and prickly pear badlands, illuminating the landscape in clean light domed by an immense cobalt sky.

—Russell A. Graves

When Texans were asked to list the ten things they liked best about Texas and the ten things they liked least, weather headed both lists.

—Peg Hein

Nobody but fools and newcomers predict the weather in Texas.

—*anonymous*

⌣

[A]ll true Texans know . . . that the only sure thing about Texas
weather is that it changes quickly, unexpectedly, and violently.

—*Betsy Noziak and Tricia Henry*

⌣

The weather of Texas is remarkable for its versatility and suddenness.
Oftenest told on this subject is the one about the farmer who started
to town in a wagon drawn by an ox team. On the way, one of the
oxen froze to death and, while he was skinning it, the other died
of sunstroke.

—Epic-Century *magazine*

⌣

The legislature convenes at Austin, near the centre of the state, and, while the representative from Rio Grande country is gathering his palm leaf fan and his linen duster to set out for the capital, the Pan-handle solon winds his muffler above his well-buttoned overcoat and kicks the snow from his well-greased boots ready for the same journey.

—William Sydney Porter (O. Henry)

When we moved to Texas from Kansas on July 15, 1994, the temperature was 110+. As I stood in my driveway watching the heat rise, I thought to myself, "Life as I know it is surely over." I didn't know the half of it. This is a great place to live—heat and all.

—Melody Kohout

There is in the Texas climate one constant—wind. It may be a waft or it may be a gale, but it never lets up. Texans seldom use the word "wind" in referring to the ever-present phenomenon. "We always have a nice breeze," they are likely to say, frequently holding on to their hats.

—*John Bainbridge*

In West Texas, on the Caprock, earth, air, fire and water blow around together in vast confounding walls of wind. . . . [T]hey say you know you been in a wind if there's no paint left on your car, if you got sand between your teeth, under your tongue and on the backs of your eyeballs, if you want to inhale water, or stay in bed all day with a paper sack over your head.

—*Susan Bright*

[W]e . . . spent every night of our first week in West Texas in Mrs. Witherspoon's storm cellar. It was March and there was no hiding place from the wind or the dust. Hailstones were big, and clouds were black, but the neighbors were kind to the frightened newcomers—and they were in the storm house too.

—*Llerena Friend*

De vedder out here I do not like. De rain vas all vind, and de vind vas all sand.

—*anonymous German pioneer farmer in the Texas Panhandle*

In some parts of Texas the wind blows quite a bit, often kicking up a lot of dust. Why once out in Lubbock the dust was blowing so hard I actually saw a rabbit digging a hole and he was six feet off the ground at the time.

—*Wallace O. Chariton*

Oh, it's dusty out here in West Texas,
In the land where the strong breezes blow,
And the ranches go by in handfuls—
Where they come from, you never know.

—*anonymous*

We have dust everywhere. Dust in the street, dust in the air, dust in the houses. The streets are filled with dust. We eat dust, breathe dust, walk in dust, sit in dust. Dust rises in clouds on every puff of air, and floats about as though it had no gravity. It settles on everything. If never before, our dusty citizens can now realize the meaning of the words dust thou art, and unto dust thou shalt return.

—*Houston* Tri-Weekly Telegraph, 1858

Blotting out every speck of light, the worst duststorm in the history of the Panhandle covered the entire region early last night. The billowing black cloud struck Amarillo at 7:20 o'clock and visibility was zero for 12 minutes.

—*Amarillo* Daily News, *April 15, 1935*

During the long Texas drouth of the 1950s a joke—probably already as old as the state—was told again and again about a man who bet several of his friends that it would never rain again, and collected from two of them.

—*Elmer Kelton*

"Hell, son, we get a total of eighteen inches of rain a year. How much more do ya want? It ain't much, but you oughta be here on the night it comes!"

—*David Carlton, quoting his Uncle Grump*

Rain! why it falls in torrents. And muddy! whopee!! If there is a town in Texas more muddy than this [Houston in 1856] pleas [*sic*] tell the Bishop not to send me to it.

—*C. H. Brooks*

We camped one night on a pretty grass plot. After night there was a Texas shower, and soon there was six inches of water in our tents; and I made my first military mental note: When you see a green spot in Texas ask why, before you camp there.

—*Colonel Percy M. Ashburn*

When you live in Texas, every single time you see snow it's magical.

—*Pamela Ribon*

The air was full of ice needles that drove into the exposed flesh and stuck, but did not seem to melt. The snow seemed to parallel the ground in its flight; yet the plains grass was covered by it in a few minutes and it rolled along the ground with the wind. That wind didn't turn aside. . . . There wasn't a hill between us and the North Pole and that wind must have come all the way—and gathering power at every jump.

—J. C. Tolman, describing 1887 Christmas blizzard in Palo Duro Canyon

On the morning of my arrival [in Houston] I was inducted into the mysteries of a "Norther," which came raving and tearing over the town, threatening, to my fancy, to demolish even the housetops. Just previous to the outbreak, the air was clear and the sun was shining, although it was cold and the wind cut sharply. A cloud-wave, like a warning herald, rose up in the north, and then the Norther himself. . . .

—Edward King

A Texas norther, my Christian friend, may be, and usually is, very much of a nuisance. . . . It is the thin edge of a northern winter which inserts itself into this earthly Eden semi-occasionally, much to our dissatisfaction. It usually catches a man seven miles from home without his overcoat. Sometimes it wanders as far south as Waco and evokes audible wishes that the Yankee would keep their d----d weather for their consumption.

—*William Cowper Brann*

If the moon could talk, it would spin a tale about Texas 'Blue Northers'—and how quickly they can whip through a city of a million people, paralyzing man and beast. As generations of Texans have said, "Son, if you don't like the weather here . . . just wait a minute . . . 'cause it'll change."

—*David Carlton*

The hurricane which visited Galveston Island on Saturday, September 8, 1900, was no doubt one of the most important meteorological events in the world's history. The ruin which it wrought beggars description, and conservative estimates place the loss of life at the appalling figure, 6,000.

—*Isaac M. Cline*

People [on the Texas Gulf coast] dated public events and incidents in their own lives by the years a hurricane struck, so long before, so long after. The big dates were 1875, 1886, and then 1900. The 1900 hurricane, widely known as "the Galveston storm," was our first experience.

—*Bertha McKee Dobie*

The people in Galveston had never held hurricanes in too much
awe. The arrival of a storm was an occasion for school to let out,
for children to slosh in the streets . . . and for crowds to gather at
the beach and watch waves crash on the shore. Thus, . . . when the
telegraphs in the weather station began ticking out a routine storm
advisory, there was little concern. . . .

—James L. Haley

You are now entering Texas.
Beware of Bull!

*—sign on a ranch fence on the Texas side
of the Red River bordering Oklahoma*

Blatant exaggeration, even outside political campaigns, has
been the oral sport of Texas, especially of West Texas, since rocks
were invented.

—Suzy Banks

Texans ignore "better," long ago forgot the useless word "good."
Everything in Texas is "best."

—*Edward Smith*

Most of all, Texans invoke their bragging rights when it comes to
the issue of size. The state's impressive land area exceeds the total
acreage covered by all of New England, New York, Pennsylvania,
Ohio and Illinois combined.

—*AAA Texas Tour Book*, 2005

It has been speculated that the only reason God invented Oklahoma
was so he would have something to put between Texas and Kansas.

—*Wallace O. Chariton*

Down deep, we still like to argue that everything is bigger in Texas, but ever since Alaska proved its claim to having more square miles of frozen tundra than Texas has prickly pear and pine trees combined, we humble Texans have had a little less to brag about.

—*Matt Peeler*

When Alaska achieved statehood Texas did not for a moment surrender its historic place in the grammar of American language and braggadociao: big, bigger, biggest, Texan. Texans argue that while Alaska is twice as large in terms of crude bulk it is Texas that remains, in more significant ways, powerful, grand and pre-eminent, the basic American metaphor for size, grossness, power, wealth, ambition, high-rolling, and boasting: in a word, Texanic.

—*Trevor Fishblock*

Saskatchewan is much like Texas—except it's more friendly to the United States.

—*Adlai Stevenson*

Texas is just one of those good-natured myths—like Paul Bunyan, George Washington's cherry tree, or Brooklyn—that has been handed down, generation after generation, until many people have come to believe that it is true.

—*Ed Creagh*

The people of other states have invented a wholly mythical Texas and proceeded to make war on it. It was unnecessary and hardly seems fair, as Texas has the rest of the country outmanned. An odd offshoot of this false image-making is the fact that Texas things and people, when they leave the state, seem to expand in size.

—*Paul Crume*

The Texas myth is the story of the cowboy and the cattleman, of the open range and the free life on top of a horse. That myth, of course, grew into a Western image that now belongs to the world, not just to Texans.

—Lera Patrick Tyler Lich

The West is the Texas of official legend, a mythical country with its straight-line horizon and flat vacant space, the Texas of hard-bellied, lean-hipped Clint Eastwoods and Gary Coopers with dark, danger-ous eyes. This is pulp magazine and paperback book Texas, Saturday matinee Texas, The cine-vérité state of celluloid heroism, six-gun valor, saloon-and-sarsaparilla true grit.

—Jerry Flemmons

The myth of Texas is undeniably masculine. Say "Texas" and what comes to most people's minds is cowboys and Indians—lusty trail drivers of the sort depicted by Larry McMurtry in his Pulitzer Prize-winning novel *Lonesome Dove*—brawny oil field workers yearning to "bring in a big'un"—football players giving their all for the glory of the team.

—*Suzanne Comer*

Myths do not just emerge full-blown, like Athena from the head of Zeus. They're made up of bits and pieces of other myths—and the Texas myth is made up of bits and pieces of the hero myth.

—*Betty Sue Flowers*

Furthermore, the Texas myth transcends itself because, in a way, it is a rambunctious brother to the American myth—the promise of a land of independence, adventure, and profit.

—*Lera Patrick Tyler Lich*

～

Most areas of the world may be placed in latitude and longitude, described chemically in their earth, sky and water, rooted and fuzzed over with identified flora and populated with known fauna, and there's an end to it. Then there are others where fable, myth, preconception, love, longing, or prejudice step in and so distort a cool, clear appraisal that a kind of high-colored magical confusion takes permanent hold. . . . One quality of such places as I am trying to define is that a very large part of them is personal and subjective. And surely Texas is such a place.

—*John Steinbeck*

～

The fact is that the old Texas is almost gone. Time and Place, those barbed wires around the regional soul, no longer bind us. . . . Nor does our history sustain us. Texans, like everyone else, find it easier to maintain loyalties to football teams and legislators than to anything so abstract as the history of a people or their literature.

—*Lyman Grant*

If Texas like Pompeii, should be buried under a blanket of ashes, and all the written records of its civilization should be lost, the scholars who unearthed the remains two thousand years later would . . . in time come to the conclusion that Texas culture revolved around something called a school. They would reach this conclusion because they would find a school building in every community from the smallest to the largest.

—*Walter Prescott Webb*

They were so much alike, those little one-room schools I had known, each looking as if it had been carelessly dropped in a cup of hills enclosing a Texas-sized pasture.

—*Stella Gipson Polk*

Rudely constructed saw horses do duty as seats for the children, and a few empty boxes secured to the walls of the room serve as desks. The blackboard is the lid to an old soap box, about 15 x 10 in. which the teacher blacked over with some of our oil and lampblack that we use for marking the sheep.

—*Elton T. Mims, quoting 1880s letter from pioneer David Williams*

I imagine [faculty members'] salaries run from $40 a month up to that of a second assistant book-keeper in a fashionable livery-stable. Judging by the salaries which they are compelled to accept, I doubt if there be a member of the Baylor Faculty, including the president, who could obtain the position of principal of any public high school in the state.

—William Cowper Brann

I had rather resign the Governor's office of Texas than to have my children studying a textbook in the public schools of Texas with Lincoln's picture left out of it, and I am the son of a Confederate soldier.

—O. B. Colquitt

Ours was a reluctant civilization. Eastland County, Texas, had its share of certified illiterates in the 1930s and later, people who could no more read a Clabber Girl Baking Powder billboard than they could translate from the French.

—*Larry L. King*

⌐∽⌐

The Board of Regents of the University of Texas are as much concerned with free intellectual enterprise as a Razorback sow would be with Keats' *Ode on a Grecian Urn*.

—*J. Frank Dobie*

⌐∽⌐

The number one priority in going to college is earning a degree, and everyone at [the University of] Texas pushes you toward that goal. They are always emphasizing academics and encouraging you to work hard in the classroom as well as on the field. Our academic staff and facilities are the best around. At Texas, everything is in place for you to focus on getting your college degree.

—*Major Applewhite*

⌐∽⌐

I don't want to send them [demonstrators in Dallas] to jail. I want to send them to school.

—*Adlai Stevenson*

Footpath, forest trail, wagon road and modern highway delineate the progression of man from primitive to higher civilization, and such progress is a characteristic of the Lone Star State, whose leading business has changed from cattle raising to a diversification of industries which bring profit and contentment to its rapidly growing population.

—*Ettie M. Doughty*

My last house is here in Texas, where I married a word processor
after a turbulent courtship. This one sits on a green bowered
shelf looking down the Colorado River. I've named it "Grass Roots"
because it symbolizes my returning to where I came from the earth
of Texas.

—Liz Carpenter

If you're fixin' to head to Texas, you'd best study up on what it means
to be tough. The quickest way to round up respect in the Lone Star
State is to demonstrate that you've got true grit.

—AAA Texas Tour Book, 2005

Texas has enough exceptionalism to last for a while yet.

—Bert Almon

Never forget, son, when you represent Texas, always go first class.
—*James Michener*

I have said that Texas is a state of mind, but I think it is more than that. It is a mystique closely approximating a religion. And this is true to the extent that people either passionately love Texas or passionately hate it and, as in other religions, few people dare to inspect it for fear of losing their bearings in mystery or paradox.
—*John Steinbeck*

Texas is a bonanza of material for a writer. We've been neck and neck with Florida for years in the Most Wacky State race, but I think the one-two combo of that psychedelic [2003] redistricting map and our hallucinogenic [2006] governor's race will put us out front.
—*Sarah Bird*

II.

MADE BY "BREATH"

The People of Texas

Texans are the only "race of people" known to anthropologists who do not depend on breeding for propagation. Like princes and lords, they can be made by "breath," plus a big hat—which comparatively few Texans wear.

—*J. Frank Dobie*

For hundreds of years, Texans have had interesting things to say about themselves, their home, and the rest of the world. For that matter, people beyond its borders have had interesting things to say about Texas and Texans for almost as long.

—*Steven A. Jent*

Residents of this state have been known in print as Texans, Texians, Texonians, Texasians, Texicans, Texanos, Tejanos and a half dozen other descriptive terms.

—*Jack Maguire*

If I had to divide the population into classes today, I should characterize a goodly number as Texians, a very large number as Texans, and finally all too many as just people who live in Texas. The Texians are the old rock itself; the Texans are out of the old rock; the others are wearing the rock away.

—*J. Frank Dobie*

A Texican is nothing but a human man way out on a limb, this year, and next, maybe for a hundred more. But I don't think it'll be forever. Someday this country's going to be a fine good place to be.

—*Frank S. Nugent*

Our imitators strive to be like us, but one thing will elude them because they may never understand *The Texan State of Mind*—that mysterious secret which also supports our remarkable individualism.

—*Ann Richards*

Texans have two pasts: one made in Texas, one made in Hollywood.

—*Don Graham*

Texans from the beginning were confronted with a dual conscious-ness; were they transplanted Americans or a new breed? Should they look to the aristocratic landed gentry for their ideals or to Rousseau's noble savage? Should their allegiance be with the Anglo-Saxon or the Spanish culture? Should they be cultivated or primitive? . . . Was the new territory they settled garden or desert? Caucasian, Christian, Yankee, Southerner, Westerner—Texans found themselves to be all of these.

—*Louis Cowan*

It was part of the Texas ritual. We're rich as son-of-a-bitch stew but look how homely we are, just as plain-folksy as Grandpappy back in 1836. We know about champagne and caviar but we talk hog and hominy.

—*Edna Ferber*

I like the people, although, frankly, I have found that people everywhere are alike. For example, you can find redneck philosophy anywhere, not just Texas. And you can find sophistication and cultivation in Texas just as well as anywhere else.

—*Amy Freeman Lee*

We [Texans] are still learning how to tell our cultural story through the lens of ordinary men and women and not just through the biographies of great men.

—*Betty Sue Flowers*

If a man's from Texas, he'll tell you. If he's not, why embarrass him by asking?

—*John Gunther*

It used to be said that there were three questions neither prudent nor polite to ask of a stranger in Texas—or, for that matter, in any frontier country of the West or Southwest "Why did you leave home?" "Where do you come from?" "Where did you get your horse?"
—*J. Frank Dobie*

It has been my consistent experience that the people of Texas are the warmest, friendliest, and best people anywhere.
—*Dee B. Whittlesey*

The friendliness of Texas folks disproves a lot of Texas jokes.
—*Marianne McNeil Logan*

He [George W. Bush] was always saying, you know, Texans are so friendly and nice, you know. He's very at home there, and he's not at home in the more intellectual, very intellectual . . . more intellectual and more cerebral. Texas is more relaxed.

—*Elsie Walker*

The houses of the early Texans were small, but their hearts were large enough to cover all deficiencies. No candidate for hospitality was ever turned away.

—*Noah Smithwick*

Texans are always excited to see other people. Even if the IRS agent arrives on your doorstep to inform you that your last five returns will be audited, you invite him in for a glass of iced tea.

—*Rosemary Kent*

Most people raised in Texas are gentle and polite and have been taught to "mind your manners" from infancy. Manners in Texas are more a matter of courtesy and respect than rules of etiquette.

—Peg Hein

Up North, I was always taught the social graces. When I moved to Texas, I found out they actually practice them.

—Dorene Badalamenti

If you're all right, Texans divine it and accept you, and unless you aren't accepted you'll never know how much that means. If you're not quite on the level, you'll just tread water in Texas and never be standing on solid ground—and money won't make the difference.

—George Sessions Perry

We learned almost all that we ever did know about practical living from our friends on the high prairies of Texas.

—Seigniora Russell Laune

When Texas was still a frontier territory, the greater part of it unknown and undeveloped, the adventurous early American settlers eagerly made their way through its boundaries with the lure of a future of wealth or of power. A restlessness born of the urge for adventure, and of necessity, led them onward through the unexplored regions as they pushed farther into the interior.

—Ettie M. Doughty

So it has been in Texas; so it is everywhere; so it must always be. It is the restlessness of the pioneer that impels him to seek fresh fields, seldom remaining to reap the reward of his toil and danger, or, if he does, he fails to take advantage of his opportunities, and old age often finds him without a place to lay his head.

—Noah Smithwick

Those who came to Texas in the early years soon found out that life was many-sided and complicated, that the needs of a pioneering community were many, and that to succeed meant hard work from morning to night. That there was no place for the laggard and loafer was soon evident.

—*Joseph William Schmitz*

Although Texas is the finest state in the union, and may be literally regarded as a "land flowing with milk and honey," it is necessary to FIRST MILK THE COWS and GATHER THE HONEY, before they can enjoy either the one or the other, for neither of them can be obtained without the aid of labor.

—*Jacob de Cordova*

Ah! there was no glare and glitter in those life-and-death struggles of the Texas pioneers.

—*Noah Smithwick*

As Texans, most of us think that we have a special, and difficult, environment with which to contend.

—*Lera Patrick Tyler Lich*

The early Texas pioneers were a hardy people. The great majority realized that only by hard work would they reap the good fortune they so ardently desired. Accordingly they began work immediately upon arrival, labored long and hard, and muttered not.

—*Joseph William Schmitz*

Not all frontier Texans who claimed perfect health really enjoyed it. Some just lied about their ills to get out of taking home remedies which were often worse than the ailment they were meant to treat.

—*Mike Blakely*

A hard road we old Texans had to travel; particularly the prairie folks, where the underground streams lay so far down under the blue clay that no one ever succeeded in digging through it, and boring for water had not been thought of. We had either to build on the lowlands along the rivers and take chances on overflows and ague or haul our water in barrels.

—*Noah Smithwick*

The shortcomings of frontier food and clothes were often considerable, but even in their most acute form they could be endured with a light heart by the settlers who were ready for hardships.

—*Joseph William Schmitz*

If you see anybody about to start to Texas to live, especially to this part, if you will take your scalpyouler and sever the jugular vein, cut the brachiopod artery and hamstring him, after he knows what you have done for him he will rise and call you blessed. This country is a silent but eloquent refutation of Bob Ingersoll's [the Great Agnostic] theory; a man here gets prematurely insane, melancholy and unreliable and finally dies of lead poisoning.

—*William Sydney Porter (O. Henry)*

The Typical Texan is a large-sized Jabberwock; a hairy kind of gorilla, who is supposed to ride on a horse. He is a half-alligator, half-human, who eats raw buffalo, and sleeps out on the prairie.

—*Alexander Sweet*

Eastern visitors were unfailingly startled at the early Texans' capacity for hard liquor.

—*Jack Maguire*

The Texan of the old regime cannot understand how it is right
that he should be taxed for the education of his neighbor's children;
neither is he willing to contribute to the fund for educating his
former bondsmen.

—*Edward King*

In the whole journey through Eastern Texas, we did not see one
of the inhabitants look into a newspaper or a book, although
we spent days in houses whose men were lounging about the fire
without occupation.

—*Frederick Law Olmsted*

Sentimentalists are still fond of saying that nature is the best
teacher—I have known many Texans who felt that way, and most
of them live and die in woeful ignorance.

—*Larry McMurtry*

We Texans have been as insular as Kansas—God save the mark.
—Walter Prescott Webb

Many hard things have been said and written of the early settlers in Texas, much of which is unfortunately only too true. Historians, however, fail to discriminate between the true colonists—those who went there to make homes, locate land, and, so far as the unfriendly attitude of the Indians permitted, resided on and improved it—and the outlaws and adventurers who flocked into the towns.
—Noah Smithwick

Texas' early frontiersmen were hardly the uncouth, gun-toting ruffians so dear to the hearts of television script writers. The majority were well educated sophisticates and most were linguists of no mean ability.

—Jack Maguire

No one estimates more highly than the writer, the intelligence, enterprise, and virtue of the present population, and yet he fully believes there were in the early history of Texas more college-bred men, in proportion to the population, than now, and as much intelligence, good common sense, and moral and religious culture among the females as among the ladies of the present day.

—*signed T.J.P. in* A Texas Scrapbook, *1875*

He who goes to Texas presuming on his own intelligence and their want of it, will find himself mistaken. I am acquainted with no community of the same number, which embodies more shrewd, intelligent men than that of the single star republic.

—*Thomas A. Morris*

Long before the Spanish explorers traveled Texas in search of gold, long before the French attempted to establish their artists' colonies in this enchanted land, long before the fathers of the Republic of Texas declared their independence from Mexico, there was another group of people who called Texas "home." They had no flag, no foreign diplomats; some didn't even have permanent houses. Still, their influence was strong and is still felt today. It was the Native Americans, the people we call "Indians," who were here long before the rest.

—Bob Phillips

So far as my observation went, the Texas Indians were unlike those of any other section of the country, subsisting entirely on meat.

—Noah Smithwick

The Texians appear to have long forgotten [the Indians] are human beings. . . . As to the idea of ever civilizing them, it never enters the brain of the settler.

—Francis C. Sheridan

If the Texans had kept out of my country, there might have been peace. But that which you now say we must live in, is too small. The Texans have taken away the places where the grass grew the thickest and the timber was the best. Had we kept that, we might have done the things you ask. But it is too late. The whites have the country which we loved, and we only wish to wander on the prairie until we die.

—Ten Bears

My mother, she fed me, carry me in her arms, put me to sleep. I play, she happy. I cry, she sad. She love her boy. They took my mother away, took Texas away. Not let her boy see her. Now she dead. Her boy want to bury her, sit by her mound. My people, her people, we now all one people.

—Quanab Parker

Resting here until day breaks and darkness disappears is Quanah Parker, the last chief of the Comanche. Died Feb. 21, 1911, Age 64 years.

      ·   *—headstone of Quanah Parker, Fort Sill, Oklahoma*

Texas history has its share of good men, bad men, and a few who couldn't make up their minds.

      —Mike Blakely

We shall rejoice when our unhappy Republic shall cease to be the arena of private feuds and disgraceful brawls, that tend . . . to degrade those who engage in them, and to fasten opprobrium upon the national character.

      —*Houston* Telegraph and Texas Register, *Jan. 19, 1842*

Tascosa has not had a man for breakfast [murdered] in all the two weeks' history of The Pioneer [newspaper]. This will be surprising news to a good many people on the outside, who thought we kept our streets always running crimson.

—*Tascosa* Pioneer, 1886

Sooner or later, a fact is going to impress itself upon you. Throughout the West, wherever there was much fighting, there were Texians.

—*Frederick Bechdolt*

You know the good part about all those executions in Texas? Fewer Texans.

—*George Carlin*

Tom Smith has been Constable of Ozona, Texas for 23 years—
and *never made an arrest or carried a gun!* Says Tom: "All I do is tell the
boys to cool off—go home and think it over—after sleeping all
night, take a good drink in the morning!—They feel so happy they
let it go at that."

—*"Ripley's Believe It or Not,"* 1935

The very qualities that made many of the Texas pioneers rebels to
society and forced not a few of them to quit it between sun and sun
without leaving cards engraved with their new addresses fitted them
to conquer the wilderness—qualities of daring, bravery, reckless
abandon, heavy self-assertiveness. A lot of them were hell-raisers, for
they had a lust for life and were maddened by tame respectability.

—*J. Frank Dobie*

When our own land forsakes us,
Texas takes us.

—old-time desperado rhyme

The Sabine River is a greater Saviour than Jesus Christ. He only saves men when they die from going to hell; but this river saves living men from prison.

—anonymous outlaw crossing into Texas
to escape American justice, 1835

In a world which in many climes is considerably discouraged, there seems to me to be markedly more starch and vinegar in the Texan outlook than in that of numerous other places.

—George Sessions Perry

We do carry guns fairly freely, and we do talk by radio on the road of life, and indigestion knows we love bourbon and beer, barbecue and chicken-fried steak, but it would be inaccurate to hold up the redneck beside the cowboy and the millionaire as a symbol of the new Texas. We are too diverse a people; we simply dwarf, in numbers and subtlety, that exaggerated and grotesque trinity.

—Bill Porterfield

For most Northerners, Texas is the home of real men. The cowboys, the rednecks, the outspoken self-made right-wing millionaires strike us as either the best or worst examples of American manliness. . . . The ideal is not an illusion nor is it contemptible, no matter what damage it may have done.

—Edmund White

In the end, perhaps, it may not be possible to escape the fact that the epitome of America is Texas, and the epitome of Texas is its most picturesque product, its millionaires.

—*John Bainbridge*

The lumberjack of the north and northwest has no counterpart in Texas mythology. Compared with the backwoods bear hunter, the cowboy, or the oilfield roughneck, the East Texas timber worker appears as drab a character as the Southern mill worker he in part resembles, tied to the region in which he, his wife, and children were born, constantly in debt to the company store.

—*Pete Gunter*

If any group in Texas has declined in influence it must be the Anglo Texans, the group most closely identified with the mystique of Texas and its images: the Alamo, the Texas Rangers, the ranchers and oil men.

—*Bert Almon*

[Texans] made their noisiest money in oil, and that's something like winning it in a crap game.

— *Harlan Miller*

Despite oilmen trigged out in suits, and wealthy wheat growers with diamond rings, the figure of respect in Texas is still the cattleman and the cattleman wants to look like a cowboy.

— *Annie Proulx*

[T]he cattlemen in Texas were the grandees of the grass, lords of the lea, and barons of beef and bone. They might have ridden in golden chariots had their tastes so inclined. The cattleman was caught in a stampede of dollars.

— *William Sydney Porter (O. Henry)*

The cattle kingdom inspired imagery and provided Texans with a worldwide identity as rash and extravagant people. Without it, other Texas stories about Rangers, gunfighters, ranchers, and Alamo heroes might have remained local legends.

—*Lera Patrick Tyler Lich*

The St. Leonard Hotel [in San Antonio] is much frequented by Texas ranchmen, some of whom are not very refined in their habits. On the staircase, at the time of my visit, a notice was displayed requesting, "Gentlemen not to spit on the floors, walls or ceilings"; and the request was by no means unnecessary.

—*Mary J. Jaques*

I once knew a West Texas cowman who had an explanation for why cowboys on scrawny range ponies often wore fancy boots, spectacular hats, and spangled chaps. "He's trying to disguise the horse," the rancher would say.

—*Paul Crume*

Come along boys and listen to my tale,
I'll tell you of my troubles on the old Chisholm Trail.
—*traditional cowboy song*

I never et much. I get up for breakfast, turn around for dinner, and go
to bed for supper. When I was riding up the Chisholm Trail the range
cooks sort of held it against me because I was a light-eating man. I've
always drunk lots of coffee, chewed plenty of tobacco, and haven't
tried to avoid any of this good Texas weather.
—*Walter Washington Williams*

We, the undersigned cowboys of Canadian River, do by these
presents agree to bind ourselves into the following obligations,
viz—First, that we will not work for less than $50 per month
and we furthermore agree no one shall work for less than $50 per
month, after 31st of March [1883].
—*declaration of cowboys' strike in the Panhandle*

•

The foreman [Colonel A. G. Boyce] of the XIT [ranch] introduced a strange practice; last Sunday he announced that six days were enough in every seven for man or beast to work, and that hereafter the XIT would observe Sunday.

—*Tascosa* Pioneer, 1888

Bose Ikard served with me four years on the Goodnight-Loving Trail, never shirked a duty or disobeyed an order, rode with me in many stampedes, participated in three engagements with Comanches, splendid behavior.

—*Charles Goodnight, for Bose Ikard's tombstone in Weatherford*

The word "cowboy" conjures up an image of the lone horseman of the plains with his six-shooter and hat. Make him a Texas cowboy and you have the mesquite, the leather and the longhorn steer.

—*Kirby F. Warnock*

Thunder of hoofs over range as we ride,
Hissing of iron and smoking of hide,
Bellow of cattle and snort of cayuse,
Longhorns from Texas as wild as the deuce;
Midnight stampedes and milling of herds,
Yells from the cowmen, too angry for words;
Right in the midst of it all I would stay.
Make me a cowboy again just for a day.

—*anonymous*

The cowboy myth came from that twenty-year period when they had no railroads from South Texas to Montana. As soon as they got railroads, they stopped doing [the cattle drive], because it was slow and cumbersome and not much fun. But that's where the romance came from.

—*Larry McMurtry*

It is surprising that . . . in this Texas, there should still exist, unknown to the vast majority of Texans and other Americans, an extraordinary type of cowboy. . . . He is Texas born and Texas bred. On one side he descends from the first Americans—the Indians; on the other, his ancestry can be traced to the Spanish adventurer and conquistador. From the mingling of these two races, a unique type has resulted—the vaquero of the Texas-Mexican frontier.

—Jovita Gonzales

Old-time cowboys would turn over in their graves if they knew that more and more cattle are wearing earrings these days instead of a brand on their hides.

—Jack Maguire

There's a line in the movie *Urban Cowboy* where Sissy asks Bud,
"You a real cowboy?" and Bud answers, "That depends on what you
think a real cowboy is." In Texas, that's a legitimate question and, I
suppose, a legitimate answer. There are lots of folks who call themselves cowboys. But I'm here to tell you that we know lots of *real*
cowboys, and, well, most folks who call themselves cowboys ain't.

—*Bob Phillips*

Today there are Japanese and Italians and even people from New
Jersey who come to Texas to see cowboys riding the range, but
nowadays most Texas cowboys ride the range in their pickups. If
you've ever wondered why they wear the brims of their hats turned
up on the sides, it's so they can sit three abreast in a pickup. And
that's the truth.

—*Peg Hein*

Texas is the most Cadillac-conscious state in the Union.

—Art Buchwald

There are, in round numbers, about twelve million of us [Texans], and I'll cross my heart and hope to burn in hell if you'll see most of us on a horse or in a Cadillac, except maybe once a year at rodeo time or when some show-off invites us to the country club. It is true that we have horses in Texas—more than ever before—but the one in every forty Texans who owns a horse is way behind the one in every ten Texans who has a pickup truck.

—Bill Porterfield

Some folks look at me and see a certain swagger, which in Texas is called "walking."

—George W. Bush

It is widely speculated that all Texans eventually go to heaven because hot air rises.

—*Wallace O. Chariton*

The boys from Texas are full of wind;
they'll tell you of their Bowie knife and
the scrapes they've been in.

—*anonymous*

Long ago we [New Yorkers] outgrew the need to be blowhards about our masculinity; we leave that to the Alaskans and Texans, who have more time for it.

—*Edward Hoagland*

Texans ain't Texans if they aren't willing to boast about the state they call home.

—*AAA Texas Tour Book, 2005*

[The Texan] has, in fact, to be a little careful not to fall into the manner of a combination train robber and rodeo hand—in a simple desire to keep people from being disappointed.

—*George Sessions Perry*

Some Texas millionaires . . . seem to suppress their natural desire to brag out loud and assume, instead, a tight-lipped smugness, which is apt to turn into a truculent uneasiness. Apparently unsure of recognition as a member of the peer group, they seem constantly on the verge of throwing aside their affected complacency, grabbing by the shoulders whoever they feel has not been properly impressed, and demanding, "Look here, don't you know who I am?"

—*John Bainbridge*

Little ol' boy in the Panhandle told me the other day you can still make a small fortune in agriculture. Problem is, you got to start with a large one.

—Jim Hightower

"Truth" in Texas is topic sensitive. If you're doing a business deal, a true Texan always stands by his word. There is nothing more sacred to Texans than their word, and they will do anything in their power to meet their obligations. But when it comes to tellin' stories, the whole truth thing blurs quite a bit.

—Jim Gramon

Outlanders never understand that the Texas tall talk is not a lie. It is the expression of the larger truth. At its most trivial, it is a tale made up by a Texan out of the goodness of his heart to entertain his friends from other states, or maybe just to improve the shining hour.

—Paul Crume

Oh, there's some sort of story telling tradition in Texas, I think, always has been, coupled with music, and probably sort of an attitude that you can do anything that you want to do.

—Guy Clark

Lots of Texans are apt to spin a tall tale on short notice, but some are prone to talking with no notice at all.

—Anne Dingus

"Tall tales" were told about the sociability of the Texans, one even going so far as to picture a member of the Austin colony forcing a stranger at the point of a gun to visit him.

—The WPA Guide to Texas

Texans, except for a coupla badduns, are honest as the day is long, and yet they'll spend a good part of that very same day lyin' to you about it. Of course their "truth" about their lyin' is that they were just "pullin' yer leg," "spinnin' yarns," or "catchin' you a whopper."

—*Jim Gramon*

Texans today watch national television rather than tell stories around campfires or the fireplace.

—*Bert Almon*

At the whittler's bench in any small Texas Town you can find at any hour of the day a man who can take a dull day in town and make it sound like the Battle of Waterloo.

The Texan applies this ennobling talent to all things Texan. Most famous Texans were big men, and they grow a little bit every time anybody tells about them.

—*Paul Crume*

You don't have to be Texan to be funny. And not all Texans are funny. But enough are to keep everybody else in stitches. It's part of our heritage—handed down from early Texans who originally hailed from somewhere else funny.

—*Ellis Posey*

I don't know why it is that Texas women are so funny. But you take Ann Richards, Liz Carpenter, and Molly Ivins. Do you know of any other state that has such comedians among their women? I imagine it is that we have so many things to laugh at.

—*Louise B. Raggio*

Because Texas men (as well as women) tend to have a funny streak, they can make fun of their own stereotypical image of being bubba, backwards, and macho.

—*Ann Richards*

The Reconstruction era has been generally recorded in history as "tragic." Historians are notoriously short of humor. The early settlers of East Texas were not. It takes spice to make a pudding remembered. The visiting carpetbaggers gave spice to life in the Piney Woods.

—*Frank Bryan*

There's only one thing worse to a Texan than poking fun at us. We'd rather be laughed at than ignored. So we poke fun at ourselves just to get back in the limelight again.

—*Ellis Posey*

In enough ways to make it interesting, Texas is a mirror in which Americans see themselves reflected, not life-sized but, as in a distorting mirror, bigger than life. They are not pleased by the image. Being unable to deny the likeness, they attempt to diminish it by making fun of it. As a consequence, Texas has become the butt of jokes too numerous—not to mention tedious to count. Still, the image remains.

—*John Bainbridge*

My favorite Aggie joke? I'm sorry I don't understand the question.
—*Lyle Lovett (Texas A&M class of 1979)*

It isn't true that Governor James Stephen Hogg had two daughters whom he named Ima and Ura as a joke. His only daughter is named Ima, but her father saw nothing amusing about it.
—*Jack Maguire*

Texans for the most part have never learned how to be dull.
—*Randolph B. Campbell*

I think Texans have more fun than the rest of the world.

—*Tommy Tune*

Like most people, Texans have a wish list. On the list you'll find they wish: the rest of the country would realize when they are joking and when they are being serious—people in the other 49 states would not assume that all of Texas is flat and desolate with only cacti and tumbleweeds for vegetation—visitors would realize the "Don't Mess With Texas" slogan is aimed at keeping people from throwing trash on the beaches and highways—and that everyone could have as much fun in life as they do.

—*Peg Hein*

You can take the girl out of Texas but not the Texas out of the girl and ultimately not the girl out of Texas.

—*Janine Turner*

Tonight my heart's in Texas
Though I'm far across the sea.
For the band is playing Dixie
And in Dixie I long to be.
Dad says some earl I'll marry,
But you have my heart and hand.
Tonight my heart's in Texas
By the silvery Rio Grande.

—traditional cowboy song

Our young bachelor friend, Comer Nettles, came in from his old home in Wichita County last Monday. He brought in a clean bunch of fifty-one head of two year old heifers in fine condition. The young man is fixing for a sure living and a pleasant home. Maidens listen to the mockingbird.

—Amarillo News, *1895*

. . . I do not suppose that in this assemblage of beauty there is to be found a decided old maid. . . . I deem it a solemn duty to inform their friends that the gentlemen of Texas have always evinced a perfect horror at the bare idea of allowing the widow, and the old maid with her pet cat, to reside long within the limits of their State.

Having first got rid of the cats, [the bachelors] obtain the necessary warrant from the county clerk, and procuring the services of a minister of the gospel or of a justice of the peace, in an almost incredibly short space of time the ladies are compelled to renounce the cheerless state of single blessedness and are transferred, without much inconvenience, to that of matrimony.

—*Jacob de Cordova*

Romance was in the air, so it was quite natural one of the handsome Turkey Track boys should toss his loop over one of our prettiest girls; wedding bells were ringing shortly after for two couples at least who were at the party.

—*Mollie Montgomery*

[S]he didn't understand the Texas way of proposing for one's hand in marriage, was what caused the fracas. She was cleaning roasting-ears for dinner when I asked her how she would like to jump into double harness and trot through life with me? The air was full of flying roasting ears for a few seconds—one of them striking me over the left eye—and shortly afterwards a young Cow Puncher rode into camp with one eye in a sling.

—*Charles A. Siringo*

Then come and sit by my side ere you leave us,
Do not hasten to bid us adieu.
Just remember the Red River Valley
And the cowboy who loves you so true.

—*traditional cowboy song*

Once I said to a Texas soldier, "You're beautiful," and he answered me, "Ma'am, you should never say that to a man."

"And what should I say to a man?"

"In Texas," he replied, "the most you can say to a man is that his pants fit him well."

—*Marlene Dietrich*

The women of Texas, like the women of every geographical division of the globe, and in every age of the world, have played their part in the drama of human progress.

—*Elizabeth Brooks*

The Texas frontier dared its women to adhere to society's rules and then threw in their way every conceivable obstacle: Indians, heat, blue northers, bugs, wind, isolation, and violence.

—*Sherrie S. McLeRoy*

In the early days of Texas, women were a great part of the effort
for Texas independence. Although mostly behind the scenes, they
also fought for hearth and home. If their men were at San Jacinto,
they were at home with guns pointing out the windows. They were
ranching women who did everything the men did, and they were
willing to live in a harsh place.

—*Kay Bailey Hutchison*

Taking all things together, the life lived by the women of Austin at
that date [1856] was a joyous, genial existence. Their chief employ-
ment appeared to be an endless tucking of fine muslin and inserting
lace in same. . . . Some of the women chewed snuff without cessation
and such women neither "tucked" nor "inserted."

—*Amelia Edith Huddleston Barr*

On one side [of the Rio Grande at El Paso] an American woman [Sarah Bowman] known as the Great Western kept a hotel. She was very tall, large, and well made. She had the reputation of being something of the roughest fighter on the Rio Grande, and was approached in a polite, if not humble manner by all of us, the writer in particular.

—*John Salmon (Rip) Ford*

Those Texas women who left a legacy as feisty, capable ranch women made clear their backbones were stronger than twine string.

—*Lou Halsell Rodenberger*

Generations of Texas women have shaped history leading with distinction and determination.

—*Anita Perry*

The Texas woman was, when I knew her, more than half a century
ago, brave and resourceful, especially when her environment was
anxious and dangerous. They were then nearly without exception
fine riders and crack shots, and quite able, when the men of the
household were away, to manage their ranches or plantations, and
keep such faithful guard over the families and household, that I never
once in ten years, heard of any Indian, or other tragedy occurring.

—*Amelia Edith Huddleston Barr*

One scrap of homemade fabric can tell us much about the realities
and nuances of a woman's life, of a community's life, in nineteenth-
century Texas.

—*Paula Mitchell Marks*

I wouldn't say that Texas women are different from all other women,
but I would say that there is a Texas trait of spirit, grit, determination,
a can-do attitude.

—*Kay Bailey Hutchison*

Texas women are true enigmas. They can be well-educated and still speak Texan, or they can wear an evening gown or Levi's to a gala and still be respected.

—*Bonnie Cerace*

Mostly, Texas women are tough in some very fundamental ways. Not unfeminine, nor necessarily unladylike, just tough.

—*Molly Ivins*

Texans are indebted to the strong, determined women who challenged society's structure and gave us role models to follow.

—*Jean Flynn*

They have been called "gentle tamers," though some of the more outrageous women of Texas would probably have disdained being called "gentle" anything.

—Sherrie S. McLeroy

But a perception exists that Texas women are different—feistier perhaps, more likely to think that anything is possible.

—PJ Pierce

I think Texas women are different from other women. Very much indeed. We are ourselves. We are not just copying somebody else. That independence shows up in both men and women. I think it is good for society.

—Sarah McClendon

The image says we are tough; reality shows us we can be vulnerable.
The legends tell of our openness; fact demonstrates we can be
closed-minded. The motto touts us as friendly; we are, though not
necessarily intimate. What we are is different—from the myths we
chase, from the other women we honor, and from one another. The
Texas Experience allows us that individuality.

—*Linda Moore-Lanning*

Texas ladies have too much history. We carry our whole lives around
on the tip of our tongues. Dancing backwards is not easy.

—*Connie L. Williams*

We are metamorphosed Texans, out of our larval cocoons with wings
pumped dry. Neither time nor space can hinder our adventures. We
are ready to fly!

—*Evelyn Cook*

Somewhere, deep down, I really feel that every Texas woman ought to own a pair of red boots—even if she never wears them.

—*Betty Sue Flowers*

Now, as an older and hopefully wiser woman, I've given myself permission to blossom like a Texas wild flower as I celebrate life, friends and books. And I've learned that floozies can still have intelligent and in-depth discussions about the books of the month even if they put on tons of makeup, dress themselves in hot pink and leopard skin prints, tease their hair and then top it off with a glittery tiara.

—*Betty Kurecka*

The ladies of Mason, bless their sweet lives,
The radiant maidens and the good queenly wives
Dress finer than any who dwell in the West
Because Smith and Geistweidt sell them the best.

—*advertisement in Mason* News, *1889*

Neiman-Marcus Co. Cordially Invite You to Attend the Formal
Opening of the New and Exclusive Shopping Place for Fashionable
Women, Devoted to the Selling of Ready-to-Wear Apparel
                    —first Neiman-Marcus advertisement
                     in Dallas Morning News, 1907

~

Texas women have had to overcome machoism, more so than other
women in this country.
                                          —Louise B. Raggio

~

Our culture today reflects that survival instinct, and you can see it in
the Mexican American woman of Texas—the Tejana. I find Tejanas
to be different from the Mexican American women in California, in
that Tejanas are much friendlier, more fun-loving, ready to party, and
more celebrative. I think we inherited those qualities from our Tejana
ancestors, who, through their camaraderie, had learned to survive the
harsh physical environment of South Texas.
                                          —Carmen Lomas Garza

~

Growing up Mexican American in South Texas shaped who I have become. I feel a pride in my people and my culture. My people have a special bond to this land; we were living here centuries before the Anglos came to Texas.

—*Irma Rangel*

I once set out in a cloud of blissful ignorance to establish my own personal list of the ten Texas women most interesting to talk to. I gave it up because the list kept growing to twenty, and then to forty and above, and I didn't know how to chop it off.

—*Leon Hale*

Texas women are like snowflakes. Individually, they might be pretty, but together, they can stop traffic.

—*Cathy Bonner*

My West Texas grandmother taught me the most important accessory for the bedroom is a reading lamp. Life is a discovery when you read a few pages of your current book, the Bible, or even a magazine story just before you fall asleep.

—*Wanda Horton*

We finish what our mothers before us start, and what we do not finish, our daughters surely will. So don't mess with Texas women— or our daughters to come.

—*Jan Jarboe Russell*

Good neighbors, sometimes I think our Maker in His Divine Wisdom, when He saw fit to create His most perfect work, selected this Lone Star State of Texas, this paradise on Earth, came here to the Second Congressional District of this Garden of Eden, and He caught the gold from the Texas sunrise and He caught the perfume from the Texas bluebonnet, our state flower, then He caught the sweetest notes from the throat of the Texas mockingbird, our state bird, molded it all together, and worked it until He made that most perfect creation of God Almighty: my mother.

—*John Henry Faulk, as Congressman John Guffaw*

And I am Texan enough that I refer to half my relatives as "sister" or "brother," even if they are really aunts and uncles. I even have an "Aunt Sister."

—*Linda Ellerbee*

Each person's life is unique, and every relationship is unique. A deep friendship (which a successful marriage is) is like one of the Hill Country oak trees—majestic, hardy, but a bit gnarled from adapting to conditions.

—Jo Virgil

One poignant example of growing up in Texas was the time I was eleven and I got my first kiss from a boy. The pre-kiss arrangements were endless. There was much discussion of time and place. It was almost like a committee meeting.

—Terrell Maverick Webb

My mother was fairly tolerant of other sects and religions. She was convinced, however, that the Lord put most of His faith in the Methodist church—specifically the Southern Methodist Church, Texas style. Methodist preachers were His favorite, most dependable messengers on Earth.

—John Henry Faulk

Non-Texas Americans find much in Texas to praise, but, adopting the traditional Old World attitude toward the New, they usually find much more to criticize. The faults of Texas, as they are recorded by most visitors, are scarcely unfamiliar, for they are the same ones that Europeans have been taxing us with for some three hundred years: boastfulness, cultural underdevelopment, materialism, and all the rest.

—*John Bainbridge*

In America, the Bostonian looks down upon the Virginian—the Virginian on the Tennesseeian—the Tennesseeian on the Alabamian— the Alabamian on the Mississippian—the Mississippian on the Louisianian—the Louisianian on the Texian—the Texian on New Mexico, and we suppose, New Mexico on Pandemonium.

—*Joseph Baldwin*

I think that, maybe, Texans are too proud. Maybe we are too loud-mouthed about it. But we're proud of our history, our heritage.

—*Marj Carpenter*

If you grow up in Texas, you develop a sense of pride early on about this state. That pride builds confidence, a can-do attitude. We know we are a little bit different and that's okay. I feel that more is expected of Texans, and therefore we are motivated to reach those expectations. The perception exists that something is a little bit different, a little bit special, a little bit bigger about our state. And we are all by birth challenged to fulfill that prophecy.

—*Jody Conradt*

Although the population has dwindled over much of the Rolling Plains, the pioneering spirit endures. In a lot of ways the people who live in this part of Texas epitomize what it means to be a Texan— tough and resilient, but most of all gracious and affable.

—*Russell A. Graves*

When you grow up on the frontier, or close to it like I did, you believe there is nothing you can't do. Texans don't seem to abide by the rules. We have a tradition that says rules are made to be broken.

—*Ann Richards*

Resistance to regulation may be stronger in drouth-prone West Texas than anywhere. This trait remains a puzzle to people in other areas, willing to trade their freedoms piece-meal for what appears to be a guarantee of security. They, perhaps, do not have this heritage of recurring struggle for survival which every succeeding generation of West Texans has had to face, each in its own time.

—*Elmer Kelton*

I am a crusader and an independent thinker, which I attribute to having grown up in Texas. Throughout our history, Texas has gone through many campaigns for what we have thought was right. We are persistent.

—*Sarah McClendon*

West Texas people, against a West Texas background, make for a beautiful thing. That the landscape is level all around makes no one really that much taller or better than the other; you are who you are.

—*Marsha Sharp*

Texan is what you are, not what you were or might be.

—*Robert Ruark*

Texans could care less who your ancestors are. Instead they ask you where you are going, what you're doing.

—*Marj Carpenter*

I doubt if any people ever had a higher appreciation—both conversationally and inherently—of original kind of characters than old-styled Texans had and yet have; ever talked more about "characters" and told more character anecdotes. And I doubt if any land ever had more genuine individuals in ratio to its population than Texas had before it began importing human sheep by the hundreds of thousands to fill up space, raise the price of real estate, and pad the census rolls.

—*J. Frank Dobie*

Traditionally, because Texans like to think they are people of energy and action, they seldom tolerate time for reflection and words.

—*Lera Patrick Tyler Lich*

Give me an army of West Point graduates, and I'll win a battle. Give me a handful of Texas Aggies, and I'll win the war.

—*George S. Patton*

Texans are risk-takers, and that is one of the things that make this state special. If they take a risk and it doesn't pay off, it's not viewed as a failure, just as a delay on the road to success.

—*Jim Gramon*

A born Texan has instilled in his system a mind-set of no retreat or no surrender. I wish everyone the world over had the dominating spirit that motivates Texans.

—*Billy Clayton*

Nor is it the habit of Texans to look back. We have a tradition of looking forward and not looking back to see where we have been or who is following us.

—*Lyndon Baines Johnson*

Texans look forward to conquering new worlds instead of wallowing in the self-pity of lost battles.

—Tumbleweed Smith

I love Texas because Texas is future-oriented, because Texans think anything is possible. Texans think big.

—Phil Gramm

I think Texans are shaped by blue skies, optimism, and more space.

—Liz Carpenter

In Texas it seemed most of the men I'd known had staked out a claim on a dream of one kind or another.

—George Sessions Perry

[L]ike longhorns, seedless grapefruit and hot-oil companies, ruggedness has thriven in Texas.

—*J. Frank Dobie*

Many people have believed that they were Chosen, but none more baldly than the Texans.

—*Edward Hoagland*

At times it seems that the people of the lesser states resent without reason the Texans' status as chosen people. They seem to blame the Texans themselves for this.

—*Paul Crume*

Here are some guidelines to help people know when they really are Texan: when they say "y'all" instead of "you guys" . . . when they hear "I was just fixin' to do that" and it doesn't sound funny . . . when jalapeños on nachos no longer make them gasp for water . . . when they learn the Texas Two-Step and the Cotton-Eyed Joe . . . and when the thought of living anywhere else makes them sad.

—Peg Hein

The individual Texan of today is as solid an American as one can find. He believes in the things of the past, because they combined to make him what he is. Confident of the future, because he knows what he wants it to be, he believes in it passionately.

—The Pathfinder (1945)

Yes, the Texan is a noble creature, fond of his mother, small children, and oil leases. It is too bad there are not enough of them to spare to other states.

—Paul Crume

III

NOT LIMITED BY FACTS

Texas History and Politics

Like most passionate nations, Texas has its own private history based on, but not limited by, facts.

—*John Steinbeck*

We Texans have a short past . . ., but it has been a turbulent, rip-snorting, hell-for-leather past, and it has made a deep impress on our lives and ways.

—*George Sessions Perry*

Texas history is as varied, tempestuous, and vast as the state itself. Texas yesterday is unbelievable, but no more incredible than Texas today. Today's Texas is exhilarating, exasperating, violent, charming, horrible, delightful, alive.

—*Edna Ferber*

In the American Southwest, we have a saying for the meaning of
the graffiti and mementos left throughout the centuries on cliff faces
and other sites by travelers and explorers. *"Paso por aqui."* "I passed
by here."

—*Sylvia Ann Grider*

In view of how Texas was later to become seamed by the trails of
multiplied millions of Spanish cattle, ranged over by countless
mustangs of Spanish blood, and dominated by men who rode
these horses, it is fitting that the very first civilized human being
to traverse it should have borne the name of Cabeza de Vaca.

—*J. Frank Dobie*

The report of Alvar Núñez Cabeza de Vaca suggested that
the greatest wealth in the New World would be found in the
central portion of today's United States. This, of course, led
to the Coronado expedition, which found nothing but sky,
grass and buffalo.

—*Jeff Carroll*

Therefore in the name of the most Christian king, Don Philip, the
second of that name, and for his successors (may they be many), I
take possession, once, twice, and thrice, and all the times I can and
must, of the actual jurisdiction, civil as well as criminal, of the lands
of the said Rio del Norte [Rio Grande], without exception whatever,
with all its meadows and pasture grounds and passes.

—*Don Juan de Oñate*

During the early 1700s the Spanish established missions in Texas and worked hard at converting the Indians to Christianity. Among the Apache and Lipan Indians, the Spanish priests found a miraculous similarity to Christianity. These Indians paid homage to the son of Unsen, the creator, said to have been killed stretched out on the crossed spines of a great cactus.

—Elizabeth Silverthorne

These Indians [at Mission San Jose in San Antonio] are today well instructed and civilized and know how to work very well at their mechanical trades and are proficient in some of the arts. They speak Spanish perfectly. . . . They go about well dressed, are abundantly fed. . . .

—Father Juan Agustin Morfi

I am already tired of the United States. It requires too much smartness, formality, politeness, dress, etc. to be considered respectable folks to suit someone who has lived in Texas as long as I have.

—*Moses Austin*

What the discovery of gold was to California the colonization act of 1825 was to Texas.

—*Noah Smithwick*

In the early days of Texas colonization, few came by wagon because there were few roads; some walked, some came on horseback. Many came by boat.

—*Jeff Carroll*

The soldiers' quarters, originally built of stone and adobe, are
almost in ruins. . . . The [San Antonio] presidio is surrounded by
a poor stockade on which are mounted a few swivel guns, without
shelter or defense, that can be used only for firing a salvo.

—Father Juan Agustin Morfi

Faulty statutes in the United States sent many a man to Texas.
Dueling was still practiced in many of the states, a trivial matter
often ending in the death of one party, the other fleeing the country.

—Noah Smithwick

Gone to Texas (or G.T.T. or GTT)

*—written on doors of abandoned houses or posted
as a sign on fences in the early 1800s*

When we want to say that it is all up with some fellow, we just say, "G. T. T.," as you would say, "gone to the devil" or "gone to the dogs."

—*Thomas Hughes*

[F]ew persons feel insulted at such a question [as to why a man has run away from the States and come to Texas]. They generally answer for some crime or other which they have committed; if they deny having committed any crime, or say they did not run away, they are generally looked upon rather suspiciously.

—*W. B. Dewees*

Another fruitful source of emigration was debt; and, while some absconding debtors took their portable property along, others gave up all and went to Texas to take a fresh start and grow up with the country.

—*Noah Smithwick*

The house was made of logs. They made a chimney to it. The door shutter was made of thick slabs split out of thick pieces of timber, and we had a large pin or peg that was drove in hard and fast, and then the Indians could not get in. . . . I was in my first Texas house and . . . I was very much pleased, and I soon got to work to make clothing for my family.

—*Mary Crownover Rabb*

Housekeepers [coming to Texas] should bring with them all indispensable articles for household use, together with as much common clothing (other clothing is not wanted) for themselves and their children, as they, conveniently can. . . .

—*Mary Austin Holley*

[Mrs. Bingham], a lady of much intelligence and good breeding, acknowledged that a change of residence to Texas had cost her a great struggle, but declared that she had since become quite reconciled to her abode, and does not feel that want of society which she apprehended. She has four or five children, and several neighbors around her, and can at any time, she remarked, pay a visit to a friend by taking a short ride of ten or twenty miles.

—*anonymous author of* A Visit to Texas, *1831*

There are no churches in Texas, no ministers of the gospel, no religious associations. Mother, I am afraid the way from Texas to heaven has never been blazed out.

—*William H. Jack, early Texan,*
in a letter home in 1836

Among the men who were laying the foundation of a nation, Stephen F. Austin, the father of Texas, was of course, the central figure. He was at that time about thirty-six years of age, though care had left an added weight of years to his appearance.

—*Noah Smithwick*

I will wear myself out by inches rather than submit to Santa Anna's arbitrary rule.

—*Stephen F. Austin*

How will things end in Texas? As God wishes them to end.

—*Manuel de Mier y Terán*

Texas has yet to learn submission to any oppression, come from what source it may.

—*Sam Houston*

The miracle of Texas lies in the fact that it is the work of a handful of men. In not a single fight during the entire period from 1800 to 1845 did they muster as many as one thousand fighting men. Overwhelming odds never discouraged them and defeat but spurred them to ultimate victory.

—*Jack C. Butterfield*

I think that Texas is forever ruined unless the citizens make a manly energetic effort to save themselves from anarchy and confusion, which are the worst of all evils. Let us march like a band of brothers.

—*William Barret Travis*

The propriety of Texas has been the object of my labors—the idol of my existence—it has assumed the character of a religion—for the guidance of my thoughts and actions.

—*Stephen F. Austin*

All I can say of the soldiers stationed here [at the Alamo] is complimentary to both their courage and their patience. But it is the truth . . . that great and just dissatisfaction is felt here for the want of a little money to pay the small but necessary expenses of our men.

—*Jim Bowie, in a letter to Governor Henry Smith,*
Feb. 2, 1836

Money must be raised or Texas is going to ruin.

—*William Barret Travis*

We Texans are prone to claim David Crockett and the other heroes of the Alamo as our own when, as a matter of fact, with the exception of seven who bore Spanish names, James Bowie was the only one among them all who had spent more than half a dozen years in Texas. Many of them were recent volunteers from the United States.

—*Jack C. Butterfield*

The blood of noble men was seeping into the ground and the bodies of heroes were lying cold in death. The last man to fall was Walker. He had often fired the cannon at the enemy. Wounded, he rushed into the room where I crouched on my cot with my baby clasped in my arms and took refuge in a corner opposite me. The Alamo had fallen and the hordes of Santa Anna were pouring over its ramparts, through its trenches, through its vaults.

—*Susanna Dickinson*

To the people of Texas and all Americans in the World—I am
besieged by a thousand or more of the Mexicans under Santa Anna.
I have sustained a continued bombardment and cannonade for 24
hours and have not lost a man. The enemy has demanded a surrender
at discretion, otherwise the garrison are to be put to the sword, if
the fort is taken. I have answered the demand with a cannon shot,
and our flag still waves proudly from the walls. I shall never surrender
or retreat.

*—William Barrett Travis, in a
letter dated Feb. 24, 1836*

Her name belongs to Texas history. She cast her lot with the
immortal heroes of the Alamo. After its fall, with the "Babe" in her
arms, she carried the news to Gen. Sam Houston at Gonzales.
*—plaque on granite memorial for Susanna Dickinson Hannig
in Texas State Cemetery*

Texas shall be free and independent, or we shall perish in glorious combat.

> —*Juan Seguin, from speech at burial*
> *of remains of Alamo defenders*

So long as there remains a State of Texas, so long as there remains a man or woman worthy of the name of Texan, so long will the names of these men [of the Alamo] shine resplendent in the flame of Memory's altars.

> —*Herbert A. White*

While we must always "Remember the Alamo" and the men who perished there, we must never forget the women who were there as well—both the survivors and the saviors later of this monument to humanities highest ideal, this shrine of liberty. The Alamo.

> —*Gale Hamilton Shiffrin*

Only Texas could turn defeat into a legend—and a song, and a tourist attraction, and a major motion picture.

—Rosemary Kent

The Alamo had fallen and its brave defenders been put to the sword. Houston was in retreat, and families fleeing for their lives. Here was a situation to try men's souls.

—Noah Smithwick

On the 12th of March [1836] came the news of the fall of the Alamo. . . . Then began the horrors of the "Runaway Scrape." We left home at sunset, hauling clothes, bedding, and provisions on the sleigh with one yoke of oxen. Mother and I were walking, she with an infant in her arms. Brother drove the oxen, and my two little sisters rode in the sleigh.

—Dilue Harris

Remember the Alamo!
> *—Texans' rallying cry as they attacked Santa Anna's forces at the Battle of San Jacinto, April 21, 1836*

For some reason, the Alamo gets publicity, and Texans are constantly reminded of a lost battle. In comparison, the San Jacinto battlefield is only seldom mentioned, yet it is at San Jacinto that Texas won its independence from Mexico.

—Tumbleweed Smith

The "runaway scrape" marked an epoch from which Texans were wont to date all events up to the time of the late war, which, of course, obliterated old landmarks, so that the rising generation probably knew but little about it; but, that they may know something of the hardships of those who wrested their heritage from the savage, I would that every survivor should lend his experience to swell the volume of history.

—Noah Smithwick

Measured by its results, San Jacinto was one of the decisive battles
of the world. The freedom of Texas from Mexico won here led
to the acquisition by the United States of the states of Texas,
New Mexico, Arizona, Nevada, California, Utah and parts of
Colorado, Wyoming, Kansas, and Oklahoma. Almost one-third
of the present area of the American nation, nearly a million square
miles of territory, changed sovereignty.

—inscription on the base of
the San Jacinto Monument

Texas, to be respected, must be polite. Santa Anna living, can be of
incalculable benefit to Texas; Santa Anna dead, would just be another
dead Mexican.

—Sam Houston

Resolved by the House of Representatives of the United States That the independence of Texas ought to be recognized. Resolved, That the Committee on Ways and Means be directed to provide, in the bill for the civil and diplomatic expenses of the government, a salary and outfit for such public agent as the president may determine to send to Texas.

—*U.S. House Committee on Foreign Affairs,*
Feb. 18, 1837

The creation of the Republic of Texas was one of the most astounding achievements of all history, a feat that in audacity of conception and brilliance of consummation is without parallel in the annals of the human race.

—*Jack C. Butterfield*

Meagre as was the honor attaching to the office of commander of
the Texas army, it must have been that which brought forward so
many aspirants for the position, which was by no means lucrative,
and fraught with difficulty, often mortification—the army going on
the principle that "the majority should rule."

—*Noah Smithwick*

I gave Dr. Branch T. Archer of Virginia a letter of introduction to
you [Sam Houston]; Dr. Archer has been in Texas upwards of twelve
months, is intimately acquainted with matters and things there, and
is in the confidence of all their leading men. He is of the opinion that
there will be some fighting there next fall, and that a fine country
will be gained without much bloodshed. . . .

—*John A. Wharton*

[Sam] Houston being elected commander-in-chief of the Texas army, his name thereafter is indissolubly intertwined with the history of the state. Though his peculiar bent did not incline toward the founding of a nation, every instinct of his nature prompted him to resistance when the life and liberties of the nation were threatened.

—*Noah Smithwick*

It's impossible to imagine the history of early Texas without the boldness and vision [Sam Houston] brought to its formative years.

—*Peg Hein*

General and Mrs. Houston were taking breakfast. [Landowner and San Jacinto veteran Jesse] Walling was at the table. He inquired: "Mrs. Houston have you ever been in Shelby County?"

The reply was in the negative.

"You ought to go there, madam. General Houston has forty children in Shelby County."

At this announcement the lady looked rather confused.

"That is, named after him," Walling added.

"Friend Walling," General Houston remarked, "you will oblige me very much by connecting your sentences more closely."

—*John Salmon (Rip) Ford*

I can regard Texas as very little more than Big Drunk's [Sam Houston's] big Ranch.

—*Mirabeau B. Lamar*

But let it not be supposed that we in Houston are going to sit down like children, and cry because we have dropped our bread and butter, although it *has* fallen on the "buttered side." Not we, nothing can be farther from our thoughts than this. We *will* have a great city, in spite of them [those who moved the capital of the republic from Houston to Austin], and if they dont [sic] behave very well up there in Austin, we will *cut off their supplies*, and throw them upon corn bread and beef.
                              —*Houston* Morning Star, *1839*

I have sworn to be a good Texan, and that I will not forswear. I will die for that which I firmly believe, for I know it is just and right. One life is a small price for a cause so great. As I fought, so shall I be willing to die. I will never forsake Texas and her cause. I am her son.
                    —*Jose Antonio Navarro, from Mexican prison in 1841*

Texans! The generous Mexican nation against which you have
offended [in the 1841 Santa Fé Expedition], as a reward to one
of your number for benefits conferred, pardons you. In his name,
which I love, I restore to you the liberty which you lost, while
invading our territory, and violating our domestic firesides.

—Antonio López de Santa Anna

During the days of the Texas Republic, duels were so common that
Texans considered such an event a mere "difficulty" or an "affray."

—Mike Blakely

The great measure of annexation, so earnestly desired by the people
of Texas, is happily consummated. The Lone Star of Texas, which
ten years ago rose amid clouds over fields of carnage and obscurely
shone for awhile, has become fixed in that glorious constellation, the
American Union. The final act of this great drama is now performed.
The Republic of Texas is no more.

—Anson Jones, Feb. 19, 1846

We surrender everything and, in reality, we get nothing, only protection.

—Sam Houston

If the principals are disregarded upon which the annexation of Texas was consummated—Louisiana was a purchase; California, New Mexico, and Utah, a conquest; but Texas was a voluntary annexation—sorrowing for the mistake she made in sacrificing her independence on the alter of her patriotism, she would unfurl again the banner of the Lone Star to the breeze and reenter upon a national career.

—Sam Houston

Of all the various boundary proposals put forward, this one which was finally adopted drew the most inconvenient and illogical line. It gave Texas a shape as peculiar as a gerrymandered county.

—Percy M. Baldwin

All new states are invested, more or less, by a class of noisy, second-rate men who are always in favor of rash and extreme measures, but Texas was absolutely overrun with such men.

—*Sam Houston*

Texas could get along without the United States, but the United States cannot, except at great hazard, exist without Texas.

—*Sam Houston*

We had to sleep on the prairie every night, six days' journey, . . . except at Goliad, and possibly one night on the Colorado, without shelter and with only such food as we carried with us, and prepared ourselves. The journey was hazardous on account of Indians, and there were white men in Texas whom I would not have cared to meet in a secluded place.

—*Ulysses S. Grant, during the Mexican War*

There is an old army story to the effect that, when General [Zachary] Taylor's little army was on the march from Corpus Christi to Matamoras, a soldier on the flank of the column came upon and fired at a [longhorn] bull. The bull immediately charged, and the soldier, taking to his heels, ran into the column. The bull, undaunted by the numbers of enemies, charged headlong, scattering several regiments like chaff, and finally escaped unhurt, having demoralized and put to flight an army which a few days after covered itself with glory by victoriously encountering five times its numbers of human enemies.

—*Richard Irving Dodge*

"Well, gentlemen," said [Sam Houston] the Senator from Texas, "as you please. There was once a boy who came home drunk to his mother, and when she scolded him, he vowed that 'they had forced it down me.' 'Pshaw,' said his mother, 'I don't believe it.' 'Well, mother,' said he, 'they were going to force it down me, and so, seeing that, I took it freely.'"

—*New Orleans* Picayune, 1848

Texas has prospered under the Union, and her interests would be better served by remaining in it.

—*Sam Houston*

Sam Houston's always been a hero to me. Tallest sculpture of an American hero. The other two taller ones are the Statue of Liberty and a saint, a religious figure in Butte, Montana. So Sam is going to get his glory, finally.

—*David Addict*

I have done all I can to keep her [Texas] from seceding. Now if she won't go with me, I'll have to turn and go with her.

—*Sam Houston*

The people of Texas are informed that in accordance with a proclamation from the Executive of the United States "all slaves are free."
—*General Order Number 3 issued by Major General Gordon Granger (1822–1876), representing Union forces occupying Galveston, June 19, 1865*

The long and arduous tale of the emancipation of Texas slaves is symbolic of the struggle of all African Americans and the day, June 19, or Juneteenth as it was known, became the commemoration and embodiment of African American freedom. . . . On Juneteenth we think about that moment in time when the enslaved in Galveston, Texas, received word of their freedom.
—*Corrine Brown*

No man ever hung in Texas by lynch law was ever half such a criminal in the sight of God or man as the man who seeks to plunge his country into a war of races, the most savage of all wars, which would result in the extermination of the blacks and the ruin of the state.

—*Houston* Telegraph *editorial*, 1868

If not curbed, [the Ku Klux Klan] will usurp the functions of the State and be destructive of government itself. It will indeed overthrow our Anglo-Saxon civilization in its relation to government.

—*Charles Culberson*

Not very long ago I was making a journey between Dallas (Texas) and Houston. In some way it became known in advance that I was on the train. At nearly every station at which the train stopped, numbers of white people, including in most cases the officials of the town, came aboard and introduced themselves and thanked me heartily for the work that I was trying to do for the South.

—*Booker T. Washington*

Dragging cannons here and there over the [Texas] Plains in pursuit of hostile Indians was about as feasible as hitting a hummingbird with a brickbat.

—Billy Dixon

O pray for the soldier, you kindhearted stranger;
He has roamed the prairie for many a year;
He has kept the Comanches away from your ranches—
And followed them far over the Texas frontier.

—epitaph on grave marker for Private Peter Corrigan
at Fort Clark, 1873

The architectural monstrosity [state capitol building] that has so long disfigured the crown of the heaven-kissing hill at the head of Congress Avenue in Austin, is no more. The venerable edifice that bore such startling resemblance to a large sized corn crib, with a pumpkin for a dome, and whose halls have so often resounded with legislative eloquence, reminding the distant hearer of a dog barking up a hollow log, is gone [destroyed by fire]. . . .

—*satirical newsletter* Texas Siftings, 1881

Now that railroads are penetrating the country, a new industry will spring up and assume surprising dimensions, and there are millions in it, Bones! Reports have it that in various parts of the Panhandle, tons and tons of these [buffalo bones] are being gathered for early sale.

—*Tascosa* Pioneer, 1887

Texas stands peerless amid the mighty, and her brow is crowned with bewildering magnificence!

—Temple Houston, dedication speech at opening of new Texas Capitol, May 16, 1888

I have no doubt [Fort Belnap] was, as I was informed it had been, the prettiest frontier post in Texas, but now [after the Civil War] desolation reigned supreme. Sand, sand everywhere; dead buffalo lying on the parade ground, a few ancient rats and bats looked on us with an evil eye for disturbing their repose, and my first night's rest in the old commissary was broken by visions of old infantry sentinels stalking ghost-like on their beat, and the wind howling through the broken roof.

—H. H. McConnell

The [Fort Inge] post was dilapidated; but the surroundings were
far more agreeable than at either Fort McIntosh or Fort Duncan.
A beautiful little river, the Leona, ran just behind the quarters, which
were built of logs, and about ready to tumble down. We moved into
a vacant house of four rooms; the kitchen was behind it, and was in
an advanced stage of decay. A high wind might easily have blown
it over.

—*Lydia Spencer Lane*

Fort Bliss seemed to be the very antithesis of its name. I met with
several officers who looked worn and melancholy. There was not the
slightest suggestion of the "loved soldier boy" in their manners or
their movements.

—*John F. Finerty*

The custom that obtains throughout the army of each officer selecting according to his rank the quarters which he may prefer, was never more fully enforced than at Fort Clark. Fifty times, perhaps, there was a general move of at least ten families, because some officer had arrived who, in selecting a house, caused a dozen other officers to move, for each in turn chose the one then occupied by the next lower in rank.

—Frances Anne Mullen Boyd

I, A. B., in the presence of these my disgruntled brethren, do most sincerely promise and swear that Old Jim Hogg is personally and individually responsible for the droughts, cyclones, hailstorms, short crops and low prices of farm products in the state of Texas; and if [George W.] Clark is elected governor he will have the country in a worse fix than Hogg has, for I do solemnly swear that Clark is a bigger liar and a smarter man than Hogg.

—John Bently Brown, proposing
alternative political party in 1892

Yesterday [railroad magnate] E. H. R. Green startled Terrell by passing through the streets in his automobile, which is the first owned in Texas. The whole town turned out to witness the sight, dogs barked, horses were frightened and one child ran screaming into the house and told her mother to come quick and see the wagon running away without the horse.

—*Dallas* Times-Herald, *1899*

Now, my boys, never after this say one and one make two, but five and one make two; one Texan and five Mexicanos. This is Rangers' arithmetic.

—*Joseph Holt Ingraham*

Imagine . . . men dressed in every variety of costume, except the ordinary uniform, armed with double-barreled shotguns, squirrel rifles, and Colt's six-shooters, mounted on small, wiry, half-wild horses, with Spanish saddles and Mexican spurs; unshaven, unwashed, undisciplined, but brave and generous men, riding pell-mell along roads, over the prairies, and through the woods, and you will be able to form a correct conception of a squad of Texas Rangers on the march.

—*Willis Lang*

Any move in the direction of effeminacy or dandyism was put down by the boys. Once on a scout between the Nueces and Rio Grande, and above the road from San Antonio to Laredo, an unlucky ranger, troubled with sunburnt and blistered nose and lips, hoisted an umbrella . . . a brisk fusillade was heard in camp. . . . [The umbrella] was shattered and torn into hundreds of pieces.

—*John Salmon (Rip) Ford*

Me and Red Wing not afraid to go to hell together. Captain Jack [John Coffee Hays] heap brave; not afraid to go to hell by himself.

—*Flacco*

⤳

I scouted, trailed Indians, suffered with cold, hunger, thirst, and witnessed many startling scenes. . . . I was one of the eleven Rangers who made the fight with forty-one Indians at the Keep Ranch, and saved the women and children there; was powder burned in the face, and one arrow cut the shoulder of my jacket.

—*Andrew Jackson Sowell*

Sometimes, there are . . . weeks when we crawl through underbrush, until our bodies are cut and bleeding; nights when we freeze, sitting so quietly waiting for a raid to take place; hours in the broiling sun, slowly walking our horses down mountainous incline; days of living in Mexican huts, eating enchiladas, frijoles and supapios prepared by Mexican cooks. Chili and more chili, keeps the backbone of a Ranger from growing flabby.

—*Alonzo V. Oden*

Sam Bass was born in Indiana, it was his native home;
At the age of seventeen young Sam began to roam.
Sam first came out to Texas, a cowboy for to be—
A kinder-hearted fellow you seldom ever see.

—*from "The Ballad of Sam Bass," anonymous author*

We are at Georgetown on our way to Round Rock to rob the bank,
the railroad or to get killed, so for God's sake be there to prevent it.
—Jim Murphy, message to Texas Rangers

~

And so he sold out Sam and Barnes and left their friends to mourn,
Oh, what a scorching Jim will get when Gabriel blows his horn!
Perhaps he's got to heaven, there's none of us can say:
But if I'm right in my surmise, he's gone the other way.
—Jim Murphy epitaph from "The Ballad
of Sam Bass," anonymous author

~

If I killed [Deputy Sheriff "Caige"] Grimes it was the first man I
ever killed.
—Sam Bass, on his death-bed in Round Rock

~

I was drafted to go out and fight with the Rangers. While I was out with the Rangers one of them lied to me and talked me into joinin' 'em. . . . He said Rangerin' was a easy life, lyin' around in camps, goin' to dances, and drawin' pay. There was no danger he said, as long as you didn't get too close to the Comanches, which was the only true thing he said. . . . We didn't go to no dances, except when the Indians was around, and then we danced lively gettin' away from 'em. . . . The horses was crowbaits, and the grub was what you could shoot with the ammunition they furnished.

—*anonymous author, Amarillo* News-Globe, *Aug. 14, 1938*

We drew a great many [Rough Riders] recruits from Texas; and from nowhere did we get a higher average, for many of them had served in that famous body of frontier fighters, the Texas Rangers. . . . They were splendid shots, horsemen, and trailers. They were accustomed to living in the open, to enduring great fatigue and hardship, and to encountering all kinds of danger.

—*Theodore Roosevelt*

To Captain John Hughes and his Texas Rangers . . . Gentlemen,—
I have the honor to dedicate this book to you, and the hope that it
shall fall to my lot to tell the World the truth about a strange, unique,
and misunderstood body of men—the Texas Rangers—who made
the Lone Star State habitable, who never know peaceful rest and
sleep . . . who will surely not be forgotten and will some day come
into their own.

   —*Zane Grey, dedication in* The Lone Star Ranger

For every line of fence lying thread-like toward the far western
horizon, every chimney of farm and ranch house, crowned by lazy
smoke; every road white across the Texas prairie—all these make
a monument to the men who rode over ahead of the settler and
homebuilder—the Texas Rangers.

   —*Eugene Cunningham*

A company of tall and grim Texas rangers strode down the streets of Amarillo. They called at the police station, left word to forward mail and rode off into the darkness for Borger to rid the famous oil boom town of the alleged vice and lawlessness which a citizens' committee and a subsequent investigation by federal and state officials declared existed there.

—*Associated Press, October 14, 1926*

The liquor traffic was broken up, many stills being seized and destroyed, and several thousand gallons of whisky being captured and poured out. Two hundred and three gambling slot machines were seized and destroyed. Numerous gambling resorts were placed under surveillance and forced to clean up, and in a period of twenty-four hours it is assumed that no less than 1,200 prostitutes left the town . . . the Mayor, City Commissioners, Chief of Police, and practically all of the Police Force of Borger resigned and were replaced by citizens pledged to enforce the laws.

—*Report of the Adjutant General of the State of Texas for the Year Ending August 31, 1927*

[Bonnie Parker and Clyde Barrow] both turned, but instead of obeying [orders to "stick 'em up"] . . . they clutched the weapons which they either held in their hands or in their laps. When the firing began, Barrow's foot released the clutch and the car, in low gear, moved forward on the decline and turned into the ditch on the left. I looked at my watch and it was 9:20.

—*Frank Hamer*

"My advice to a peace officer is to be honest and clean," [A. E. Bennett] said, puffing on his pipe and looking at the well-worn .45 semiautomatic he had carried for so many years as a Ranger and then as a Special Ranger. "If you're honest, it won't make any difference if you're tough."

—*Mike Cox*

24 hours is not enough for a day; when I get control of the universe I'm going to make the day 35 hours long so I'll have time enough to get my [Rangering] work done and drink a cup of coffee now and then.

—*E. M. (Pappy) Davenport*

At some point—there is no known record of when it happened or who did it—a Texas Ranger, perhaps following the request in [George C.] Childress's resolution [in the Republic of Texas] that officers and soldiers of the army wear a star, fashioned a homemade badge of authority by taking a Mexican silver coin and cutting a star in it. . . . The resulting icon, which has become known as the star-in-a-wheel badge, took on a double symbolism: Since Texas had just been wrested from Mexico by Anglo-Americans and native-born Tejanos, a star cut from a Mexican coin represented a near perfect metaphor.

—*Mike Cox*

Boys, I've killed fifty-two men and one woman. I killed them all right and I go to sleep every night knowing I did right.

—*Frank Hamer*

Seldom can a people's history be profoundly changed by a single event on a single day. But Texas' entrance into the industrial age can be linked directly to the discovery of oil at Spindletop, three miles from Beaumont, on Jan. 10, 1901.

—*Texas Almanac, 2006–2007*

The oil industry produced a business born for Texas. The discovery of oil at Spindletop set free the entrepreneurial spirit of wildcatters, leasing agents and speculators.

—*Max Brown*

When the [Santa Rita No. 1 oil] well was first being dug [in 1923], some Catholic investors had laughed and suggested that it be named after the Saint of the Impossible. Santa Rita was the well, its top suddenly transformed into a fluttering, Salome's veil of oil, that truly opened up Midland and the rest of endless, empty West Texas. . . .

—*Bill Minutaglio*

There were nodding pump jacks and pivot irrigation rigs . . . to the left and right, condensation tanks and complex assemblies of pipes and gauges, though such was the size of the [Panhandle] landscape and their random placement that they seemed metal trinkets strewn by a vast and careless hand.

—*Annie Proulx*

Texas, through the last half of the twentieth century, has suffered little "history." There has been enormous growth and . . . economic development, which are not the same thing.

—*T. R. Fehrenbach*

The ferocity with which the Texas establishment fought to maintain mastery of the [post-World War II] economy and the political landscape seemed continually tied, either directly or tenuously, to race. Even when not debated openly, it was the elephant in the parlor of every political discussion.

—James L. Haley

The emergence of Texas into the modern world was presided over by farmers, and not by businessmen.

—T. R. Fehrenbach

He's the natural. If I can ever get [Lyndon Johnson] on the ticket, no way we can lose. We'd carry Texas. Certainly I want him.

—John F. Kennedy, discussing candidates
for vice president, 1960

Dallas is a very dangerous place. *I* wouldn't go there. Don't *you* [John F. Kennedy] go there.

—*J. William Fulbright*

It all began so beautifully. After a drizzle in the morning, the sun came out bright and clear. We were driving into Dallas. In the lead car were President and Mrs. Kennedy, John and Nellie Connally, a Secret Service car full of men, and then our car with Lyndon and me and Senator Ralph Yarborough.

—*Lady Bird Johnson, diary entry for November 22, 1963*

I heard the shots. I had an awful feeling but I couldn't truthfully say I knew they were gun shots—until I looked at the President. Then I knew he had been shot. I heard all three shots. John [Connally] just heard two. He didn't hear the one that hit him.

—*Nellie Connally, recalling events of November 22, 1963*

You can't say Dallas doesn't love you!
> *—Lady Bird Johnson, to President Kennedy*
> *just moments before shots rang out*

My God! They've shot the President.
> *—Senator Ralph Yarborough,*
> *in motorcade Nov. 22, 1963*

[It was] impossible for me to re-create the thoughts and emotions that surged through me during the forty-five terrible, interminable minutes that we spent in Parkland Hospital.
> *—Lyndon Baines Johnson, recalling*
> *events of November 22, 1963*

In the mid-1960s, Texas was in a wary, precarious mind-set, unsure how to distance itself from the lingering impressions left behind by Lee Harvey Oswald, Jack Ruby, and all the other players and scenes that had emerged several months earlier on Commerce Street, in the Texas Theatre, inside Parkland Hospital in Dallas.

—*Bill Minutaglio*

Called "Two-Gun Ollie" by Larry King, this Texas-born Marine [Oliver North] charged up Capitol Hill, "told off Congress right to its teeth," and corralled the masses into believing that the "Wild West syndrome" must manifest itself if we are to master the monsters of this world.

—*Jeri Tanner*

[Gov. Rick] Perry says Texans have been so gracious and giving [to Hurricane Katrina evacuees], and he's really proud of the citizens of the state.

—*Associated Press, September 2005*

In the end—the ostensible end [of the Enron trial] being May 25
[2006]—the Enron verdict [guilty for both Jeff Skilling and
Ken Lay] was like the death of a close relative who had long ago
been diagnosed as terminal: inevitable but still shocking in its power
and finality.

—Mimi Swartz

Most writers in Texas couldn't give a hoot about historical Texas,
and many readers (like me) often find the idea of Texas either
unimportant or distracting.

—Lyman Grant

The great difference between Texas and every other American state
in the twentieth century was that Texas had a history.

—T. R. Fehrenbach

Texas politics is proof you can fool all the people most of the time.

—anonymous

Take the unsavory stew of MacBeth's witches, season with ipecac, perfume with asafetida, and you get an *olla podrida* resembling Texas politics.

—William Cowper Brann

Naturally, when it comes to voting, we in Texas are accustomed to discerning that fine hair's breadth worth of difference that makes one hopeless dipstick slightly less awful than the other.

—Molly Ivins

A friend once suggested that Texans must like political jokes because they keep electing so many of them to office.

—*Wallace O. Chariton*

The Texas system threw up men who instinctively could make the correct political decision, but only rarely a great moral decision.

—*T. R. Fehrenbach*

The definitive statement on Texas political ethics—source unknown, but often quoted by Texas liberals—is: "If you can't take their money, drink their whiskey, screw their women, and vote against 'em anyway, you don't belong in the Legislature."

—*Molly Ivins*

It has been said the state of Texas installed flood lights on the state capitol building so no politician could steal the dome.

—Wallace O. Chariton

Volumes could be filled with accounts of the knavery, the double-dealing, the cross purposes, the perjury, the lies, the bribery, the alteration and erasing, the suppressing and destroying of papers, the various schemes and plots that for the sake of the almighty dollar have left their stains upon the records of the [Texas] General Land Office.

—William Sydney Porter (O. Henry)

I have seen similar bodies at the North: the Federal Congress; and the Parliament of Great Britain, in both its branches, on occasions of great moment; but none of them commanded my involuntary respect for their simple manly dignity and trustworthiness for the duties that engaged them, more than the General Assembly of Texas.

—Frederick Law Olmsted

I carry no special brief for government—many years of studying the Texas legislature will disenchant anyone.

—Molly Ivins

In Texas, politicians often use the longhorn-type speech. That's one which has two good points, but they are a long way apart with a lot of bull in between.

—Wallace O. Chariton

For years, people had said that the demanding and crafty [Bob] Bullock would be the next old-school Democratic governor of Texas. Instead, his last dramatic act was to embrace the Republican son of the former president—and watch as the Republicans took every statewide office for the first time since Reconstruction.

—*Bill Minutaglio*

Actually, most people in Texas is plumb Republikin ignernt. Yessir, Republikin ignernt. Wouldn't know a Republikin if they met it standing in the middle of the road.

—*John Henry Faulk, as Cousin Claude*

We didn't have a GOP here [in Midland] then. Elder [George H. W.] Bush was one of the first precinct chairmen. He won us over because we're just a real friendly bunch of people.

—*Rosenelle Cherry*

The Texas Legislature consists of 181 people who meet for 140 days once every two years. This catastrophe has now occurred sixty-three times.

—*Molly Ivins*

There were still lingering suggestions about the elder Bush being a latter-day northeasterner dispatched to Texas by the family; it was all there, said some people who watched him, in the way he carried himself, in his inability to convince Texans that he was more than a "plucky lad," as one Texas writer would later describe him in his inability to consistently behave in a grittier, homespun, Lone Star way.

—*Bill Minutaglio*

He'll tell you he's a Texan / Though he's got those Eastern ways / Eatin' lots of barbecue / With a sauce that's called béarnaise.

—*Mark Russell, during George Bush's
1980 presidential campaign*

I am delighted to be here with you this evening because after listening to George Bush all these years, I figured you needed to hear what a real Texas accent sounds like.

—*Ann Richards, 1988 keynote address*
at the Democratic National Convention

Down at the state capital in Austin they have some mighty smart folks and some mighty dumb ones. The problem is nobody can tell 'em apart.

—*Wallace O. Chariton*

In Texas, we do not hold high expectations for the [governor's] office; it's mostly been occupied by crooks, dorks and the comatose.

—*Molly Ivins*

I don't know of any other state where the governor has less
authority than the lieutenant governor. The governor's office
is more of a cheerleader and a p.r. person . . . veto power and
making appointments, that's about their duty.

—*Paul Rea*

A Texas governor has only two happy days: the day he is inaugurated
and the day he retires.

—*Joseph D. Sayers*

Dear Governor:
You run things up in Austin and I'll run 'em down here.

—*Roy Bean*

There's no one in Texas better prepared than I am to be governor. If I run for it, I want it. If I want it, I get it. And if I get it, I'll be the best damn governor ever.

—*T. Boone Pickens*

And the state of Texas, when I was governor, we built an awful lot of prisons. And to be frank with you, I made a deal, and the deal was that I would help pass the legislation and be for building a lot more prisons in Texas if I could get rehab programs for people who were alcoholics and drug abusers because I knew that over 80 percent of the crime committed in Texas was committed by people under the influence of alcohol or drugs.

—*Ann Richards*

They like her [Ann Richards'] hair, but they're not strongly anchored to her.

—*Karl Rove*

If I run, I'll be the most electable. Absolutely. No question in
my mind. In a big media state like Texas, name identification
is important. I've got it.

—*George W. Bush*

[George W. Bush] has always been a political person. He would walk
in that room and work it. Even as an eighth-grader, and that's pretty
foreign to a juvenile—to even think that that is important.

—*Doug Hannah*

[George W. Bush] lit out for the plains of West Texas. This is part
of the American West. It is a throwback to an earlier era where
people were judged by the content of their character and not their
curriculum vitae.

—*Karl Rove*

I view Texas as a way of life, a state of mind, a way to think. . . . I don't want Texas to be like California. . . . I was a small businessman. . . . I believe everybody should be held responsible for their individual behavior. All public policy should revolve around the principle that individuals are responsible for what they say and do. . . . Our leaders should be judged by results, not be entertaining personalities or clever sound bites.

—*George W. Bush, campaigning for governor of Texas*

George sort of did leap into it [a race for Congress], but even back then he was smart enough to know that a lot of politics was simply timing. You know, there are a lot of would-be governors of Texas sitting around today who never took the opportunity to get into a race when the time was right. If George [W. Bush] is good at anything, it's timing.

—*Laura Bush*

Dynasty connotes inheritance. Nothing is inherited in Texas politics.
—*George W. Bush*

[Being a shareholder in the Rangers baseball team] solved my biggest problem in Texas. . . . My problem was "What's the boy ever done?" I have to make a fairly big splash in the pool in order for people to recognize me. . . . The advantage is that everybody knows who I am. The disadvantage is that no matter how great my accomplishments may be, no one is going to give me credit for them.
—*George W. Bush*

The joy is in Texas but our hearts are in Florida.
—*George H. W. Bush, following sons George W.'s victory and Jeb's loss in gubernatorial races in 1994*

For the last thirty years, our culture has steadily replaced personal
responsibility with collective guilt. This must end. The new freedom
Texas seeks must be matched with renewed personal responsibility.
—*George W. Bush, inaugural speech as governor, 1995*

Save us from the federal government, Texans can run Texas, we don't
need any help from the federal government.
—*George W. Bush, as governor of Texas*

There is a role for government, but government can't make people
love one another. I will tell you this: I would sign into law, I would
sign the law, or I'd spend all the money it took in our budget to cause
people to love one another. I wish I knew the law that would make
people love one another . . . 'cause we'd pass it in Texas.
—*George W. Bush, as governor of Texas*

Midland is probably where he [George W. Bush] first got the
mistaken idea that doing well in business is the solution to
America's problems, that is, what's good for business is good
for America. "Opportunity and business fortune for all" isn't really
true for everyone, . . . but it was for them [the Bushes].

—*Randall Roden*

Vote early and vote often. That's the way we do it in Texas.

—*Barbara Bush, in Florida during
son Jeb's 1998 gubernatorial race*

As governor of Texas, I have set high standards for our public
schools, and I have met those standards.

—*George W. Bush*

Texas: 32 electoral votes, another of the so-called big enchiladas or if not an enchilada at least a big taco.

—*Dan Rather*

This [U. S. Senate primary] race is not a matter of life or death for me. If I lost by one vote [to Lyndon Johnson] in an honest count the heavens wouldn't fall in. But about half a million Texans voted for me and they have been defrauded and robbed.

—*Coke Stevenson*

Texans should not be taxed on our taxes.

—*Kay Bailey Hutchison*

The rule was that girls never ran for [student council] president at Austin High—only vice-president. Well, I reversed that order, and I asked a cheerleader friend of mine—a male—to be my running mate.

—*Carole Keeton Strayhorn*

. . . John Nance Garner of Uvalde . . . once said he "gave up the second most important job in the government for one that didn't amount to a hill of beans" when he moved from Speaker of the House to Vice President.

—*Jimmy Banks*

The Vice-Presidency of the United States isn't worth a pitcher of warm spit.

—*John Nance Garner*

. . . Texas is . . . a place that is very patriotic. And there is this notion that if the country is at war, the Texans rally behind it.

—*H. W. Brands*

Most "foreigners" find it difficult to understand why only a few men have dominated the Texas political scene during recent years but the answer is relatively simple. While most of them have been conservatives, all of them have had dynamic personalities. . . .

—*Jimmy Banks*

Good thing we've got politics in Texas—finest form of free entertainment ever invented.

—*Molly Ivins*

IV

AN ARMY
WITH
BANNERS

Texas Sports and Recreation

Sectional football games have the glory and the despair of war, and when a Texas team takes the field against a foreign state, it is an army with banners.

—*John Steinbeck*

But why, some say, the moon? Why choose this as our goal? And they may well ask why climb the highest mountain? Why, 35 years ago, fly the Atlantic? Why does Rice play Texas?

—*President John F. Kennedy,*
speaking at Rice University in 1962

If you want to surf, move to Hawaii. If you like to shop, move to New York. If you like acting and Hollywood, move to California. But if you like college football, move to Texas.

—*Ricky Williams*

Football is to Texans what religion is to a priest.

—*Tom Landry*

I'd heard about Texas football and how much of a religion it is, but to go to Odessa and experience it first-hand is something different than just hearing about it.

—*Jay Hernandez*

The rest of the world is sweeping past us. The oil and gas of the Texas future is the well-educated mind. But we are still worried about whether Midland can beat Odessa at football.

—*Mark White*

Whatever we thought of football, it was the defining sport in our town. During Coach [Joe] Golding's fifteen-year tenure, Wichita Falls was a high school dynasty.

—*Jan Reid*

[Texas football is] an in-the-trench battle. It's meat on meat, flesh on flesh, and stink on stink. And that's the only way you can play it. Maybe you'd better scratch out that stink on stink. Somebody might not like that.

—*Darrell Royal*

We're going to have to do something about this guy [Roger Staubach]. He's going to ruin the image of an NFL quarterback if he doesn't start smoking, drinking, cussing, or something.

—*Don Meredith, referring to the quarterback of the Dallas Cowboys*

There is a great winning tradition at [the University of] Texas. That's what I always loved about the Yankees. You either loved or hated the Yankees. Everybody had an opinion about them. UT football is the same way.

—*Mack Brown*

America's Team

—*Bob Ryan, applied to the Dallas Cowboys first in 1978*

We [Dallas Cowboys] had some talented players, but just not enough of them. We were a lot like an oil slick; we came from everywhere but we weren't very deep.

—*Tom Franckhauser*

Tom Landry is a perfectionist. If he was married to Racquel Welch, he'd expect her to cook.

—*Don Meredith, referring to the coach of the Dallas Cowboys*

To all Texans, football—high school, college, and professional—is a way of life. Some people believe the main reason there is a public school system is to give Texans more football teams to root for.

—*Rosemary Kent*

I kept a list [of skeptics' remarks]. It was an old competitive habit that went back to my childhood in Plano, when I'd never had as much money as the other kids, or played the right sport. (They didn't force you to play football in Texas, but they sure wanted you to.)

—*Lance Armstrong*

And in our state if you are kin by blood or marriage to a linebacker, or an offensive tackle, or a member of the pep squad, the law is that you go to the games and you root for the team. You may need to drive halfway across Texas to do your rooting, but you have to go and root.

—*Leon Hale*

I am not decrying football—I incline to the view that an occasional rough-and-tumble scrapping match in which there is imminent danger of black eyes, and even of broken bones, is good for a boy. I simply point out that as an intellectual game it not only ranks below chess, billiards, and baseball, but does not even rise to a parity with pugilism.

—*William Cowper Brann*

Don't fear to compromise your sex by attending the baseball game. It is affirmed on the best authority, that Mrs. Cleveland, now the first lady in the land, is enthusiastically devoted to the game. That should make it fashionable, and insure the game financial success in Texas.

—*Austin* Statesman, *1889*

I've seen them wear six-shooters to games in the Texas League, and when a fan pulled one out in Fort Worth and took a shot at a fly ball, I was ready to check out.

—*"Wild Bill" Setley*

As the older George Bush immersed himself in Zapata [Petroleum Corporation], in Republican politics, his first son [George W.] was trying to memorize the starting lineups of every major-league baseball team, collecting baseball cards in a shoebox, and mailing the cards to players who might autograph them.

—*Bill Minutaglio*

[George W. Bush] wasn't playing first base [in Midland's Little League], he wasn't that talented. . . . Well, actually he wasn't a good hitter.

—Frank Ittner

⁓

I just want people when they say "Texas Rangers" that they think here's a group of people trying to improve somebody's life . . . it's not called motherhood, apple pie and baseball for nothing . . . it's not called motherhood, apple pie and track.

—George W. Bush, as part owner of the Texas Rangers baseball team

⁓

As owner of the Rangers, he [George W. Bush] is anchored in the minds of Texans as a Texas businessman. It gives him instant exposure and identification.

—Karl Rove

⁓

Even before there were teams for women to play on, I believe Texas women possessed those qualities that would make them winners, regardless of scoreboard measures.

—*Jody Conradt*

I love it [practicing golf in Texas]. You can find anything. You can practice rain, you can practice wind, you can practice on hard pan, you can practice on lush golf courses, you can find all the conditions you will ever encounter in Texas.

—*Tom Kite*

Coaching at the University of Texas, I encountered a lot of west Texas boys. West Texas boys were well known for their strong grips, which they develop because they play in the wind so often. They can hit a 7-iron so far you can't believe it.

—*Harvey Penick*

[W]hen it is all said and done, when the drives no longer have the carry they used to, when the iron shots are not as crisp as they once were, and the 29 putts per round are now more like 33 or 34, the one thing that we all have learned from Harvey [Penick] is love. A love of a game that teaches us more about ourselves than we sometimes care to know. And a love of the people that we share this game with.

—*Tom Kite*

Very few teachers in golf have had [the essential art of communication], as Harvey [Penick] does, and I think that it would be safe to say that it requires a gift from Above. I know that Harvey has spent a considerable amount of his lifetime teaching golf [in Texas], not thinking of *what* to say to a pupil, but *how* to say it.

—*Ben Crenshaw*

Ben [Crenshaw] is one of the greatest players of all time, a natural. When he was a boy I wouldn't let him practice too much for fear he might find out how to do something wrong.

—*Harvey Penick*

For me, Harvey [Penick] reduced golf, as he did life, to a few sound, irrefutable, worthwhile principles. And he expressed those principles in simple unadorned, down-to-earth, and often humorous terms.

—*Betsy Rawls*

I'm so happy, I'm gonna buy the Alamo and give it back to Mexico.
    —*Lee Trevino, after winning his first major golf tournament*

Out here in West Texas, we make our own fun, and goat-roping's our golf game.

—*Art Roane*

Some days I don't even want to put shoes on. I just want to wander around barefoot, dragging the cuffs of my jeans in the Texas grass, and think about nothing more complicated than whether to drink a beer or play golf, or both.

—*Lance Armstrong*

If God had intended Texans to ski, he'd have made manure white.

—*old Texas saying*

Texans know the best way to while away a summer afternoon is by keeping cool as they bob along in an inner tube on a river that only sometimes rushes.

—*Sophia Dembling*

You are not in a hurry there [on the Brazos River]; you learned long since not to be.

—*John Graves*

[T]he river is a splendid place to paddle. The slow, flat stretches [of the Guadalupe River] give you a chance to drink in the scenery, while the river's falls and rapids promise heart-pumping action. Plus, the spring-fed Guadalupe always feels cool in the dog days of summer.

—*Jack Lowry*

One of the greatest things about hiking and backpacking in Texas is that you can choose exactly what appeals to you, rugged mountains or thorny deserts, the shorelines of placid lakes or flowing rivers, sandy beaches, or the pine-hardwood forest of East Texas.

—*Mildred J. Little*

A bicycle is the long-sought means of transportation for all of us who have run-away hearts. Our first bike is a matter of curb-jumping, puddle-splashing liberation; it's freedom from supervision, from carpools and curfews.

—*Lance Armstrong*

The true meaning of America, you ask? It's in a Texas rodeo, in a policeman's badge, in the sound of laughing children, in a political rally, in a newspaper . . . in all these things, and many more, you'll find America. In all these things, you'll find freedom. And freedom is what America means to the world. And to me.

—*Audie Murphy*

A Texas rodeo (pronounced "roadie-oh") is a field day for cowboys—a sort of cowpunchers' Olympics.

—*Rosemary Kent*

Pari-mutual wagering means lots of jobs. Texas needs pari-mutual betting. Besides, that way we don't have so far to drive.

—*Bum Phillips*

Crabbing was more a family matter than a party. The method was to tie a piece of salt pork on one end of a string and drop it into water where crabs were plentiful—the River, the Intracoastal Canal, or best of all, Stubblefield Lake, a pinched-off bend of the Brazos River.

—*Bertha McKee Dobie*

I have fished for crawdads with a string and fatback in a mud tank on the way to North Zulch; I have barrel-raced at Snook, and I have drunk sour mash whiskey from a water glass in a dance hall in Rocksprings. But the most Texas thing I ever did was swim the Navasot on horseback during a flood.

—*Ann Melvin*

I go out to a place called Dead Man's Hole, and I stare down into it, and then, with firm intent, I strip off my shirt and I leap straight out into what you might call the great sublime. . . . Dead Man's Hole is a large green mineral pool gouged out of a circular limestone cliff, so deep into the hill country of Texas that it's hardly got an address.

—*Lance Armstrong*

You see a bass stirring in shallow water about fifty feet downstream, up against a brushy bank. You get some line flying, and more line, and a little more, and there's no wind and you don't hang up on willows behind you, and when things feel right you release and the line rolls across the water and the fly plips onto the surface in exactly the spot you hoped for, and the fish hits it. . . . I just need to make that perfect cast, and get the strike.

—*Leon Hale*

Some of the biggest fish in Texas are caught by the tale.

—anonymous

～

In Texas, the fish seem to grow the most between the moment they strike a lure and the instant they spit it out.

—Wallace O. Chariton

～

When Texans start talkin' huntin' or fishin', strap on your waders, 'cause it's gonna get deep in a hurry.

—Jim Gramon

～

Got up early and went deer hunting with [brother] Tom. Rode about nine miles "thro' brush and brake" but saw very little game—no deer at all. We brought home some squirrels and partridges. The ride, thro' the fresh, dewy morning hours! Oh, that was worth something! Everything looked as if it were "made over." The sky had that wonderful blueness I have never seen anywhere but in San Antonio; the hillsides were green with the tender green of spring and there was a perfect blaze of flowers everywhere.

—Mollie E. Moore Davis

My only chance was to make a good shot. The bear was not more than forty feet from me and was coming right on. I pointed my gun toward her, but now I had what Texans called "buck ague." I was so scared that for the life of me I could not hold my gun steady, as I pointed it toward the bear. I had faced cannon before, but never had I felt as I did while I was facing that bear.

—Z. N. Morrell

As one of the last habitats of wild bobwhite quail left in the nation, the Rolling Plains plays host to hunters from all over the country who want their chance to chase the 6-ounce winged rocket.

—*Russell A. Graves*

In my high school years I went on a quail hunt or two, mainly as an observer because there would be four or five boys and only one shotgun. The method of hunting was to find a covey of birds and blast into them, on the ground, and see how many you could get with one shot. I don't remember doing that myself but I watched it done, and I would have done it if I had ever gotten a turn with the gun.

—*Leon Hale*

I feel safer on a racetrack than I do on Houston's freeways.

—*A. J. Foyt*

I'm more careful riding my bike around Austin. These days I travel with somebody following me in a car, or on a motorbike, to help shield me from the trucks, the rocks, and the cranks in their pickups.

—*Lance Armstrong*

[M]ost of my small-town contemporaries [in Archer City] spent their high school years trying desperately to be good athletes, because the attitude of adults had them quite convinced that their sexual identity depended upon their athletic performance.

—*Larry McMurtry*

Some of Texans' favorite pastimes include wearing cowboy boots, telling Aggie jokes, going to any kind of football game, hunting anything that's legal and two-stepping around a sawdust-covered floor.

—*Peg Hein*

I didn't understand it [the welcome-home reception in Austin].
I was just another Austin bike geek who liked his margaritas and his
Tex-Mex, and Americans weren't supposed to care about cycling.

—*Lance Armstrong, after his first*
Tour de France victory in 1999

It's always good to spend some time in a town where the major
concerns of the day are when and how much it's gonna rain, the
Friday night football score, and what kind of price cattle are
bringing down at the auction barn.

—*Bob Phillips*

Now that President Bush doesn't run anymore, he rides his mountain
bike fanatically. People wonder why he stays at the [Texas] ranch so
long. It might be the mountain bike trails.

—*Lance Armstrong*

V

CELEBRATION OF LIFE

The Events and Amusements of Texas

The Stonewall Peach Festival is the real thing. It's a celebration of life in the Texas hill country, of the harvest, of the indescribably delicious peaches, of the reward of hard work and the sheer fun of rodeoing, of cold-beer drinking, of washer pitching, of barbecue eating, and of pretty-gal watching.

—Cactus Pryor

Talk around campfires is so common that some Texans think it's a law, and maybe it oughta be. The campfire tradition is alive and kickin' at the Kerrville Folk Festival. The festival attendees, referred to as Kerrverts, gather in the evenings and have singarounds until the wee hours.

—Jim Gramon

Running of the Bull. . . . The event's name may evoke visions of the notorious chase of man by beasts through the streets of Pamplona, Spain, but this West Texas festival, held in what the promoter proudly claims is the "Capital of Nowhere" [Eldorado], celebrates not the bull of hoof and horn, but the bull of fib and fabrication.

—*Suzy Banks*

You have to wonder what's most impressive about the . . . WORLD'S LARGEST RATTLESNAKE ROUND-UP, in Sweetwater: the fact that a community of farmers and ranchers devised a way to turn all their diamondback-infested nooks and crannies into ripe hunting grounds, drawing crowds from as far as Australia for the pleasure of ferreting out the area's pests, or that somehow each year, the Miss Snake Charmer Scholarship Pageant prompts a handful of sweet-faced teens to prove their merit pre-roundup by hacking off a bunch of rattlesnakes' heads and skinning the bodies. (Try that, Miss Texas.)

—*Katy Vine*

For four days every June, downtown San Antonio comes alive with the faces, flavors, and sounds of people whose roots can be traced from Vancouver to Vladivostok. . . . The Texas Folklife Festival . . . was created to show the countless cultures of Texas to the world.

—*Jack Lowry*

The Texas Scottish Festival reminds me of an extended family reunion, enlivened by brawny men in kilts tossing the caber, slender red-headed lasses dancing the Highland fling, plates of shepherd's pie, classes in whiskey tasting, and, above all, nonstop music. Of course, here men wear kilts with cowboy boots. . . .

—*Eileen Mattei*

A lot of cities in Texas stage festivals in October, featuring beer, sausage, and oompah bands. But not Marshall. That city has an October spectacular that revolves around the fire ant.

—*Tumbleweed Smith*

[M]odern Texas history started with the celebration of the Texas Centennial, because it was in 1936 . . . that the rest of America discovered Texas.

—*Stanley Marcus*

Smells of mesquite smoke permeate the air as dedicated barbecuers prepare what they hope will be the winning brisket. It's a Saturday morning in mid-May, deep in the heart of Texas, and my husband and I are at the World Championship Bison Cookoff in Santa Anna.

—*Lou Ann Dean*

While not all Texas dishes have their own cook-offs, luckily the competitions are sufficiently broad and numerous to provide a mother lode of new culinary prizes.

—*Barry Schlachter*

Only in Texas would a classical music festival be called the Texas Toot! What about an event called the Prickly Pear Pachanga? Or a favorite of mine, the Big Stinkin' International Improv & Sketch Comedy Festival, referred to by everyone as BS.

—*Jim Gramon*

Texas beauty contests are the human equivalent of cattle auctions.

—*Rosemary Kent*

Playing dolls gave way to more sophisticated diversions; summer revivals, the annual lyceum course, and the Chautauqua, that educational lecture series held each summer in a tent that brought us culture. The Chautauqua tent at Vernon was probably no larger than that at Electra, but it seemed so when we drove there for important programs, including hearing William Jennings Bryan deliver his speech on "The Cross of Gold."

—*Llerena Friend*

A practical joker around an office in a city is now apt to be held in thorough contempt. Not so in the country. I think the practical joke ranks near the top as an entertainment medium in rural Texas.

—*Leon Hale*

One of the favorite diversions of the old rangers was to make a newcomer believer that the state furnished the rangers with socks and start him off to the captain's tent to demand his share of the free hosiery. The captain took these pranks in good part and assured the crestfallen applicant that the rangers were only playing a joke on him, while his tormentors enjoyed his discomfiture from a safe distance.

—*James B. Gillett*

You won't find a mechanical bull at Billy Bob's [honky-tonk in Fort Worth]—they have the real live thing right inside the club, twistin', snortin', buckin', and stompin', Texas-style.

—*Matt Peeler*

When young [Texas] folks danced those days, they danced; they didn't glide around; they "shuffled" and "double shuffled," "wired" and "cut the pigeon's wing," making the splinters fly.

—*Noah Smithwick*

One of the entertainments given the old Rangers was a dance. Some of us had never seen modern dancing. An old Ranger who sat by Captain Roberts was very much shocked, and as the dance progressed kept remarking to the Captain, "Now ain't that scandalous?"

—*Mrs. Dan W. A. Roberts*

Square dancing is the ideal foreign relationship. An Irishman can enjoy a dance with a Greek. I heard a man from Scotland say: "You can't fight a man you've danced with."

—*Tumbleweed Smith*

SECOND TO NONE

TO NONE

The Flora and Fauna of Texas

From the cathedral stillness of the Big Thicket to the land across
the Pecos River, from Padre Island to the big sky of the High Plains,
from the waters of the Hill Country to the timbered bottoms of the
fabled Blacklands, Texas has a native flora that, in sheer loveliness,
is second to none.

—Benny J. Simpson

The devil was given permission one day
To make him a land for his own special sway.
He scattered tarantulas over the roads,
Put thorns on the cactus and horns on the toads;
He lengthened the horns of the Texas steer
And added a foot to the jack rabbit's ear.
He hung thorns and brambles on all the trees,
He mixed up the dust with a million fleas.
He quickened the buck of the bronco steed,
And poisoned the feet of the centipede.
The heat in the summer's a hundred and ten,
Too hot for the Devil and too hot for men.

—anonymous

I have known really fierce animals like the ground squirrel or the West Texas mouse to lose their wildness and beseech human aid when afflicted with a goathead burr. This burr not only hurts when it hits. It later produces a kind of cold shivering like the sting of a red ant.

—Paul Crume

Tumbleweeds, worn small by a winter's thrashing, rolled across the road in the hundreds. Sheets of plastic, food wrappers, sacks, papers, boxes, rags flew, catching on barbwire fences where they flapped until a fresh gust tore them loose. The [Panhandle] landscape churned with detritus.

—Annie Proulx

Plum picking harkens back to the earliest recorded days of the plains of Texas, Oklahoma and Kansas, where wild plums grow voluntarily in moist soil. For Indians and settlers, the tart fruits were wild-growing desserts and a necessary part of the diet.

—*Staci Semrad*

When the sun rises high in April, East Texas becomes a land adorned with flaming colors. A fish jumps in a spring-fed lake, its crystal clear water reflecting a wooded hillside and a blue sky.

—*Tumbleweed Smith*

[M]y dad taught me to never let external forces bend you against your will. He was a firm believer in being your own person, and when I was young, he wouldn't let me follow the trends and the fads of the other kids. He wanted me to be my own person, and I take that from the dogwood. You can't bend dogwood against its will. It'll snap and break.

—*Dean Price*

It is impossible to imagine the beauty of a Texas prairie when, in the vernal season, its rich luxuriant herbage, adorned with its thousand flowers of every size and hue, seems to realize the vision of a terrestrial paradise. . . . The delicate, the gay and gaudy, are intermingled with delightful confusion, and these fanciful *bouquets* of fairy Nature borrow tenfold charms when associated with the smooth verdant carpet of modest green which mantles around them.

—*Mary Austin Holley*

The founding of the National Wildflower Research Center
[in Austin] was my way of repaying some of the debt for the
delight and sustenance Nature has given me all my life.

—*Lady Bird Johnson*

Every spring the roadsides and hills over a large portion of Texas
become a rhapsody in blue as the bluebonnets open.

—*Peg Hein*

The edges of the [Panhandle] road were misty with purple-flowered
wild mustard whose rank scent embittered the air.

—*Annie Proulx*

They struck across a world carpeted with an endless reach of curly mesquite grass. The [wagon] wheels made no sound. The tireless ponies bounded ahead at an unbroken gallop. The temperate wind, made fragrant by thousands of acres of blue and yellow wild flowers, roared gloriously in their ears. . . .

—William Sydney Porter (O. Henry)

When spring comes to the Big Thicket, mud gets hub deep,
the sweet gums and loblollies stand erect, and Carolina wrens
sing proudly.

—Tumbleweed Smith

In Central Texas, lavender farms have not only sprouted but taken root, and each year, the list [of growers] grows longer. . . .

—Ann Gallaway

During autumn months, in an area that stretches from Texarkana to Woodville, elms and hackberries sport cloaks of gold deepening almost to orange. Black gums and sumac are blushing in crimson, and sweet gums are turning gold to red.

—*Tumbleweed Smith*

The tarpon . . . is obviously a Texan. Like other Texans, he is a trusting, friendly soul; and he often gets hooked by some outlander. When this happens, the tarpon, in typical Texas fashion, calls attention to himself. He rises in the air like a rocket and dances on his tail while the blue mist shines around him. He looks ten times as big as he is.

—*Paul Crume*

It seemed as if all the coyotes and wolves that roamed these vast solitudes had collected, and taken their position on the hills around our camp, to serenade us with dismal howls and yelps.

—*A. J. Sowell*

The moon is low and the wind is still. The lovely stars, the 'forget-me-nots of the angels,' which have blossomed all night in the infinite meadows of heaven, unheeded and unseen by us poor sleepy mortals for whom they spread their shining petals and silvery beams in vain, are twinkling above in all their beauty and mystery. The lonely cry of the coyote is heard mingling with the noise of a piece of strong Texas bacon trying to get out of the pantry.

—*William Sydney Porter (O. Henry)*

Though [the jackrabbit] is common to the entire Southwest, we look upon him as a Texas invention, are proud of how fast he can run and how long his ears are.

—*George Sessions Perry*

Carrying a weight of one hundred and fifty to two hundred pounds, [mules] would follow a scout of Rangers on the dead run right into the midst of the hottest fight with Indians or desperadoes. They seemed to take as much interest in such an engagement as the Rangers themselves.

—*James B. Gillett*

A few days out from Corpus Christi the immense herd of wild horses that ranged at that time between the Nueces and the Rio Grande was seen directly in advance of the head of the column and but a few miles off. The column halted for a rest, and a number of officers [in Zachary Taylor's army], myself among them, rode out two or three miles to see the extent of the herd. As far as the eye could reach to our right, the herd extended. To the left it extended equally. There was no estimating the animals in it. I have no idea that they could all have been corralled in the State of Rhode Island or Delaware, at one time.

—Ulysses S. Grant

Buffalo came and went like a mighty torrent. They covered the prairies as far as the eye could see. When moving rapidly, they made the earth tremble under their hoofs.

—Robert Mayfield, describing buffalo herd in 1884

One of the greatest curiosities ever open to the free gaze of the San Antonio public, was an armadillo, which was hauled about the streets yesterday on a countryman's wagon. The man found the animal while cutting wood in Atascosa county, and brought it in with the intention of selling it to some curiosity seeker. . . .

—*San Antonio* Express, 1879

The rats. Golly, there were so many of them that at one time, that summer of 1926, the Rig Theater [in Borger] offered a bounty on rat tails. For ten or twelve rat tails, you could get admission into the theater.

—*W. Horace Hickox*

There are alligators in the Big Thicket too. For certain there is at least one, which escaped its pen in the Alabama and Coushatta reservation in the spring of 1970 and meandered down into Big Sandy Creek. I am sure many of the Indians would have liked to go with it, to get away from the tourists.

—*Pete Gunter*

Ranchers and allergy sufferers may not appreciate the Hill Country's short-stature juniper forests, but two endangered songbirds do: the golden-cheeked warbler and the . . . black-capped vireo.

—*Elaine Robbins*

A singer of a distinctive type; a fighter for the protection of his home, falling if need be in its defense, like any true Texan.

—*Texas legislature adopting mockingbird as state bird, 1927*

The great prairie dog cities of the short-grass plains which once covered hundreds of square miles [in the Panhandle] were gone, but some old-fashioned red-tails [hawks] continued to hunt as their ancestors, in flat-shouldered soar, turning methodically in the air above the prairie, yellow eyes watching for the shiver of grass. Many more had taken up modern ways and sat atop convenient poles and posts waiting for vehicles to clip rabbits and prairie dogs.

—Annie Proulx

The brown pelicans taught us DDT was a poison. It killed the brown pelicans, almost demolished 'em on the Texas coast. That's our front line. If it hadn't been for those brown pelicans, we might have been next.

—Ted Appell

East Texas has its own distinctive sounds: A crow calls across a valley on a foggy morning. A squirrel chatters. The trees muffle the sounds as they ripple through the woods.

—Tumbleweed Smith

During World War II, millions of Texas free-tailed bats faced the prospect of being drafted by the U.S. Army. They were to carry incendiary bombs into enemy territory.

—Jack Maguire

Remember this: A fire ant loves to die. Dying is its purpose for being. Because as quick as you smash it, it is reincarnated as two fire ants instead of one. This is what I think. My belief has not yet been supported by all the fire ant research going on at public expense. But I bet it will be, in the end.

—Leon Hale

VII

PROCLAIMING INDIGENOUS DISHES

The Food and Drink of Texas

Texas does not, like any other region, simply have indigenous dishes. It proclaims them. It congratulates you, on your arrival, of having escaped from the slop pails of the other 49 states.

—*Alistair Cooke*

My first meal on Texas soil was dried venison sopped in honey. After having spent some months in New Orleans, where everything of the known world was obtainable, it looked like rank starvation to me, but I was adaptive.

—*Noah Smithwick*

One day's drive is just like another—breakfast of coffee, biscuit, and bacon, at six o'clock, the men doing the cooking by turns, if we have no regular cook. Then the herd is started.

—*Alex E. Sweet and J. Armoy Knox*

We ran out of food, and, compelled to strike camp and there being
no settlements near and no game but wild horses, the very thought of
eating which sickened me, there was a prospective famine, at least for
me. The other boys had been in Texas long enough to get rid of any
fastidious notions about clean and unclean beasts, so when provisions
ran out they killed a mustang and were provisioned for a siege.

—*Noah Smithwick*

Supper consists of tea or coffee, warm cornbread and fried bacon.
These articles of food are always found, but in the better inns biscuits
are served hot in addition to eggs, butter, honey and canned fruits.
The hostess, or at least some feminine member of the family, sits
at one end of the table and serves the tea. This is done in the most
dignified and solemn manner. The cups are passed in silence, and
later repassed in the same manner to be refilled.

—*Ferdinand von Roemer*

My little sisters . . . and I found many small things to interest us on the [Velasco] prairie and its verges. We rubbed prickly pear fruits in the "dirt" to remove thorns so that we could eat them. We nibbled peppergrass and sheep sorrel to get their bite on our tongues. The best of the wild growths that only children considered edible was a small red fruit we called wild cranberry. It did not taste at all like cultivated cranberry, and I have no idea what it was.

—*Bertha McKee Dobie*

Food-wise we ranged from the sublime to the ridiculous, sometime having such delicacies as homemade hominy, or wonderful catfish from the Navasota River. In the winter Papa and Uncle Shed killed the hogs, and that meant that we would be eating ham, backbone, porkchops, hogshead cheese, sausage, chitlins . . ., and liver and lights. Cold weather was the time Papa went possum hunting. If he trapped one he would pen it up and feed it well—almost make a pet of it—and expect me to eat it at one of his famous possum suppers.

—*Terrell Maverick Webb*

No one loves chicken-fried steaks more than Texans. It is another one of those recipes that will never quite compare with what a particular Texan grew up on.

—*Barry Schlachter*

I know I belong to a Texas country church, because the only time I lock my car or pick-up in the parking lot is during the summer so my neighbors can't leave me a bag of squash!

—*Anne Terry*

We had all we could eat and give away of tomatoes, Rocky Ford cantaloupes, and the plainer vegetables that were "so good for us." People who have never stood in a tomato patch and eaten a tomato picked ripe from the vine and dipped mouthful by mouthful into salt held in the left palm have no idea how good a tomato can be.

—*Bertha McKee Dobie, recalling her childhood in Velasco*

One of the sweetest things about summer in Texas is taking a bite
from a luscious, ripe peach you picked fresh off a tree or plucked
from a pile at a farmer's market, and letting the juice dribble down
your chin.

—*Kathryn Jones*

Keep in mind that Texan vegetarians are as rare as Valley ocelots.
—*Dan Rather*

Forget al dente vegetables. Texas food is home-cooking with a
vengeance—heavy, fattening, plentiful. . . . This "love on a plate
and lard in the skillet" school of cooking is not even close to
nouvelle cuisine—if you can see your plate at the beginning of a meal,
you simply haven't taken enough.

—*Rosemary Kent*

Ask any Texan from Dalhart to Brownsville to describe Texas food, and you'll get as many answers as there are miles (or armadillos) between the two cities.

—*Stephan Pyles*

Nothing is better on a hot East Texas summer day than an RC cola and a bear track, which is a hard gingerbread bar with white or pink frosting on top.

—*Leatha Dailey Glisson*

The highest sales of lard in the United States are in the Hispanic neighborhoods of West Texas. It's always been a part of Tex-Mex, and in some recipes, it's irreplaceable.

—*Robb Walsh*

Tex-Mex may have had a negative connotation at one time, but today we recognize it as a unique cuisine that developed as the cultures crossed the border over and over again. It's neither Southern cooking, nor Mexican cooking, but a blend of the two that became something totally different.

—*Shannon Gelrich*

Fajita is the Spanish diminutive for belt or skirt, and the term refers to the four strips of diaphragm muscle on a steer. Because the word applies specifically to cattle, there's really no such thing as chicken or shrimp fajitas, regardless of what your favorite restaurant's menu says.

—*John Morthland*

To the goggling unbeliever [Texans] say—as people always say about their mangier dishes—"but it's just like chicken, only tenderer." Rattlesnake is, in fact, just like chicken, only tougher.

—*Alistair Cooke*

In Texas, beef reigns supreme. (Where else would you find a monumental bronze sculpture of a herd of steers?) The preferred cut of meat for barbecue is brisket and the preparation is almost Zen in its simplicity, consisting chiefly of time and wood smoke.

—*Steven Raichlen*

This smokin' thing is getting out of hand. The custom of cooking meats over wood fires has been going on since before there was a place called Texas, but in recent years the concept has gotten so refined and peculiar that nobody here can agree with anybody else about anything.

—*Joe Nick Potoski*

It has been said that Texas is a place where they barbecue everything except ice cream.

—*Rosemary Kent*

Of the world's four great cuisines—French, Italian, Chinese and Texan—only the later has a recipe beginning, "First, dig a three-foot-deep hole. . . ."

—*Jerry Flemmons*

What would a chuckwagon dinner or a true Texas barbecue be without a plate of beans?

—*Barry Schlachter*

Chili packs a wallop stronger than a spurned lover sending a four-knuckle message to his romantic rival. If Texas had a state condiment, it would no doubt be Tabasco.

—AAA Texas Tour Book, 2005

By this time you're thinking that not even a politician can louse up Texas chili any worse than putting green bell peppers and kidney beans in it. Well, you're wrong. Get a good grip because here comes the final transgression. I hope you're ready: Sen. [Kay Bailey] Hutchison put into her chili four tablespoons of mole sauce.

—Leon Hale

Chili tastes different in Texas, where its preparation is a serious undertaking and arguments can ensue over just what needs to be included. One thing that's not is beans. That's a separate dish.

—Barry Schlachter

[Chicken-fried steak is] an over-ordered dish in Texas, and most of the time it's really nothing you'd want to write home about.

—*Richard (Kinky) Friedman*

You can have your coq au vin and your chicken Kiev; make mine King Ranch chicken. A comfort food good enough to feed polite company.

—*Barry Schlachter*

There is no consensus on what Tex-Mex means in Texas, either. Middle-aged Anglos tend to describe Tex-Mex as a specific sub-set of the larger genre of Mexican food—one that involves yellow-cheese enchiladas with chopped raw onions and chili gravy, as served in San Antonio around 1955.

—*Robb Walsh*

Hopkins County stew was made from what was available. The basics were corn, potatoes, and tomatoes. You had to have a little meat in there, and it didn't matter what kind. You'd shoot a squirrel and have squirrel stew. You could kill your neighbor's chicken or a buzzard or anything you could get.

—*Henry Sartain*

Oh, I've dined off the golden plates and fine silver of the crowned heads of Europe, and I've et pheasant under glass, but nothing can beat a plate full of Texas barbecue down here with the people of Pear Orchard.

—*John Henry Faulk, as*
Congressman John Guffaw

My kitchen, like my inner compass, spins between two places. Most days I operate a San Antonio kitchen. There is homemade salsa in the refrigerator and a pot of beans on the stove. However, [my children] can tell when my mood has turned dark and sad, toward Cleveland [Texas]. They come home to find black-eyed peas, cornbread, and mustard greens on the table, served with a main dish of overcooked roast beef.

—Jan Jarboe Russell

Nobody is going to make biscuits as good as a Texan's own mother.

—Barry Schlachter

Hamburgers, that most iconic of American foods, couldn't be more
Texan. . . . [Fletcher] Davis opened a lunch counter in the late 1880s
[in Athens, Texas] that served ground beef between two slices
of bread. When he took his creation to the 1904 World's Fair
in St. Louis, he was the hit of the midway, and the burger took off
from there.

—*John Morthland*

[T]here is as much difference between a Texas hamburger
and one made in the East as there is between Sam Houston
and Calvin Coolidge.

—*George Sessions Perry*

Texas cowboys do eat quiche; they just don't call it that. . . .

—*Barry Schlachter*

Now's the time to heed the call of the pecan trees surrounding the Crockett County town square, in Ozona, where a nutritious snack is free for the taking. Sort of. First, you have to beat the squirrels to the bounty. Second, pecans are usually plentiful only every other year. And third, the Algonquins didn't call them *pacane*—which means " nut too hard to crack"—for nothing.

—*Suzy Banks*

The English get homesick because they cannot get gooseberries and "arf and arf" and Lea & Perrin's sauce, growing on every mesquite in Texas. They forget to give any credit to the watermelons, the figs, and other good things that they get in Texas, and that they could not raise, even in a hothouse, in England.

—*Alexander Sweet and J. Armoy Knox*

VIII.

PIECED-TOGETHER PORTRAIT

The Music and Art of Texas

Like a giant patchwork quilt, Texas music is a pieced-together portrait of the Lone Star State and its people. It is a lively mix influenced by the variety and backgrounds of all the folks who have come to Texas over the years.

—Rosemary Kent

Once again, the stars at night were big and bright. And deep in the heart of Texas, the music world celebrated the best and brightest from yesterday, today and tomorrow.

—Nick Brandon, reviewing the 2006
South by Southwest Music Festival in Austin

During the cattle drives, Texas cowboy music came into national
significance. Its practical purpose is well known—it was used
primarily to keep the herds quiet at night, for often a ballad sung
loudly and continuously enough might prevent a stampede.
However, the cowboy also sang because he liked to sing. . . . In this
music of the range and trail is "the grayness of the prairies, the
mournful minor note of a Texas norther, and a rhythm that fits the
gait of the cowboy's pony."

—The WPA Guide to Texas

I once punched cattle on the T-Bar Ranch. As we followed a long
string of white-face cattle across the bed of an old alkali lake
reflecting the moon's light, while the wind swept across the plains
and the coyotes howled from the head of Laguna Rica, I wanted
to answer the forces of nature, and did answer them, in wild, half-
maniac compositions of my own. In such times and for such reasons
as these, ballads are born.

—R. L. Smith

[T]he chief contribution made by white men of Americas to the folk songs of the world—the cowboy songs of Texas and the West—are rhythmed to the walk, the trot and the gallop of horses.

—*J. Frank Dobie*

I'd bet that among Texans who take an active interest in music, there are ten country and Western fans to each person who prefers popular or classical fare. I can't prove that. I just bet that way.

—*Leon Hale*

Lone Wolf, chief of the Kiowas, was invited to an entertainment at Mangum on Sunday. For his special benefit one of the ladies gave a favorite selection on the piano. The noble red man listened patiently until she had finished when he said: "May-be-so me go, me sleepy."

—*Quanah* Tribune, *1894*

Rock-and-roll is plain old West Texas honkytonk music. It has been taken out of the poolrooms and the shabby Saturday-night dance halls, but it is the same music, with the same squirmy rhythm, the same baying-at-the-moon style of singing.

—*Paul Crume*

I got treated very badly in Texas. They don't treat beatniks too good in Texas. Port Arthur people thought I was a beatnik, though they'd never seen one and neither had I.

—*Janis Joplin*

My father [Groucho Marx] is not very clear about the exact phrase-
ology of some of these insults [from a Nacogdoches crowd in 1920],
but he does remember calling the Texans in the audience "damned
Yankees" and throwing in a couple of lines that went something like:

> Nacogdoches
> Is full of roaches.

And:

> The Jackass
> Is the finest
> Flower of
> Tex-ass.

—*Arthur Marx*

If you'd a' told me when I got out of high school—I did get my
ABCs through the twelfth grade—that I'd be writin' poetry of any
sort sixteen or eighteen years later, I'd a' looked at you like you
didn't have any more sense than a stomped duck.

—*Dennis Gaines*

Mr. [J. Frank] Dobie claimed that the Texas mockingbird sounded just as sweet as the British poets' nightingales and larks. He said that lyric poetry was beautiful wherever it was created.

—*John Henry Faulk*

We [Texas novelists] are country writers yet, but country writers who have moved to the city to write. . . . The emotions, images, symbols that animate our books pertain to the country still.

—*Larry McMurtry*

Those writers fortunate or unfortunate enough to be born in Texas must live with two gigantic images: the fantasy world of cowboys, Indians, and rich oilmen and the real world of hardship, subsistence, and stagnation.

—*Lera Patrick Tyler Lich*

I am the first and only serious writer that Texas has produced. These young people may turn out to be first rate. The woods are swarming with writers. In all this ferment, we're bound to get some good ones. But so far I am the only one. If you can show me the others, I'll be glad to see them!

—*Katherine Anne Porter*

From [Larry] McMurtry's blending of . . . remembered and imagined worlds comes fiction of unusual strength, poignancy, and realism. His eleven novels published between 1962 and 1987 attest to the potency of both personal experience and the Texas myth.

—*Lera Patrick Tyler Lich*

A viny, tangled prose would never do for a place so open; a place, to use Ross Calvin's phrase, where the sky determines so much. A lyricism appropriate to the Southwest needs to be as clean as a bleached bone and as well-spaced as trees on the llano. The elements still dominate here, and a spare, elemental language, with now and then a touch of elegance, will suffice.

—*Larry McMurtry*

Regional values addressed in [Larry McMurtry's] novels penetrate regionalism, becoming a fictional ethology. And dilemmas faced by both McMurtry and his characters are common to many people, not just Texans.

—*Lera Patrick Tyler Lich*

I didn't want to be regarded as a freak. That's what they all thought about women who wanted to write.

—*Katherine Anne Porter, explaining why she left Texas*

"The Cowboy," one of the best sculptures of its kind in existence, stands today on the Capitol grounds in Austin. Strangely enough, it was done by a woman from New York who knew little of the West and was living in Paris at the time.

—*Jack Maguire*

Houston is the art car capital of the world, and it was decided that if there was going to be an art car museum, it had to be in Houston.

—*Brian Taylor*

IX

BUBBA'S
THESAURUS

The Sayings, Lingo, and Superstitions of Texas

Forget that Roget fella—here in Texas we're more apt to consult Bubba's thesaurus. In Texas, folks aren't just rich—locals say they didn't come to town two to a mule. Someone doesn't merely die— she opens herself up a worm farm. A scoundrel is "greasy as fried lard"; a summer day is "hotter than a fur coat in Marfa."

—Texas Monthly *review of Anne Dingus's*
More Texas Sayings Than You Can Shake a Stick At

Need a Texas-ism to describe the heat? No sweat. There are dozens of steamy similes for summer suffering (not surprisingly, there are far fewer for winter weather). How hot is it? It's hot as the hinges of hell; hot as a two-dollar pistol; hot as a stolen tamale.

—*Anne Dingus*

Long before daily around-the-clock weather reports became available, a West Texas housewife knew from hard-earned experience the truth of the West Texas saying: "It's bad luck to hang your clothes out on the line if there is a bank of blue haze in the west." The bad luck is, of course, what happens to freshly washed clothes still wet on the line when a dust storm hits.

—*Kenneth W. Davis and Everett Gillis*

There's a saying in Big Spring: "No, this isn't the end of the earth, but you can see it from here."

—*Stephan Pyles*

Texas has four seasons: drought, flood, blizzard, and twister. That old saying isn't far from wrong. Because of its sheer size, Texas experiences all kinds of weather—sometimes all at once. Out in West Texas, the weather can be drier than the heart of a haystack and windier than a fifty-pound bag of whistling lips. A duststorm is dubbed "Panhandle rain."

—*Anne Dingus*

A West Texas rain: a sandstorm.

—*Boyce House*

[T]he smell and an immediate choking sensation in his throat as he drove past an enormous feedlot, the cows obscured by the manure dust that loaded the wind and was clearly the source of the cloud, introduced him to the infamous brown days of the Texas panhandle, wind-borne dust he later heard called "Oklahoma rain."

—*Annie Proulx*

Say you're an expatriate who just moved back to Texas. Upon your return, you might be "happy as a hog in slops" or "happy as a boardinghouse pup."

—*Anne Dingus*

Then there was the cowboy who was feeling so happy, he shouted: "I can whip a rattlesnake and give 'im the first bite!"

—*Boyce House*

I should explain here that in East Texas parlance the term Nervous applied with equal accuracy to anything from chronic nail-biting to full-blown psychosis.

—Mary Karr

A damn independent boy, independent as a hog on ice.

—Sam Rayburn

Although not the driest region in Texas, much of the Rolling Plains gets only a couple of feet of rainfall annually. As the saying goes, "You should be here the day we get it. . . ."

—Russell A. Graves

Away up on the plains in the Texas Panhandle is the city of Amarillo, 3,500 feet above sea-level. An old saying is: "There's nothing between Amarillo and the North Pole except a barbed wire fence." . . . And when it's especially cold, say, around Austin, down in the middle of Texas, you are sure to hear the remark: "Somebody musta tore down Amarillo's fence."

—Boyce House

Everybody to their own taste, said the old woman as she kissed the cow. (An East Texas saying passed down from my grandmother to my mother and then to me and my sister.)

—Martha Ragsdale

We have a saying in Texas: The rooster crows, but the hen delivers the goods.

—Jim Hightower

Dogie—a calf whose mammy has died and whose pappy has run off with another cow.

—*Boyce House*

The herds of some of the early-day cattlemen in Texas increased rapidly, perhaps by branding animals belonging to others. Of such a ranchman, it might be remarked, "His cows always have twin calves."

—*Boyce House*

The [Ranger] captain was "as taciturn as a turtle in a drought—until he gets to knowing you."

—*Lubbock* Avalanche-Journal, *June 22, 1941*

Of Captain Bill McDonald, renowned Texas Ranger, it was said:
"He would charge hell single-handed with a bucket of water."

—*Boyce House*

Everybody invited and nobody slighted!

—*frontier invitation to a cowboy dance*

There never has been a horse that can't be rode or a cowboy that
can't be throwed.

—*old cowboy saying*

I've got as much chance as a stump-tailed bull in fly time.

—*anonymous*

The sun has riz, and the sun has set, and here I is in Texas yet.

—*anonymous*

Texas land is so poor it takes twenty years to rust a nail.

—*anonymous*

Texas land is so rich you can plant a crowbar at night and harvest tenpenny nails in the morning.

—anonymous

The weather in Texas shows that God has a sense of humor.

—anonymous

There's an old expression that Texans use when talking about the state's ever-changing weather: "If you don't like it now, just wait five minutes."

—Texas State Travel Guide, 2004

You can always tell a Texan, but you can't tell him much.

—anonymous

When Pat Neff ran for governor on a "bone-dry" platform, he declared he was going to make Texas so dry "that a man will have to prime himself before he can spit."

—Boyce House

Don't mess with Texas.

—Texas Department of Transportation slogan

Where the West Begins

—Fort Worth city slogan

The word "maverick" is used to describe a person who makes his own rules, someone who marches to his own beat.

—Peg Hein

Galloping dominoes: dice

—Texas slang

Mexican canary: burro

—Texas slang

Mexican gasoline: tequila

—Texas slang

Hoover beef-steak: jack-rabbit.
—common saying in Texas during the Depression

Hoover hog: armadillo
—common saying in Texas during the Depression

[John W. (Bet-a-Million)] Gates erected a barbed wire fence on San Antonio's Military Plaza and filled it with 50 rough and tough Longhorn steers. Then he bet the assembled ranchers $100 against $10 that the fencing which is "lighter than air, stronger than whiskey and cheaper than dirt" would hold the steers against anything.

—*Jack Maguire*

Back in the 1540s when Coronado and his Spanish army of adventurers crossed these endless plains in search of gold, he thought he might get lost. So he had his men drive stakes into the ground to mark the way. To this day, this area is known as the Staked Plains or the *Llano Estacado* as it is called in Spanish.

—*J. Evetts Haley*

The word we use with ourselves is *mojado*. It means "wetback." Or *immigrante ilegal*. "Illegal immigrant." But usually we say "wetback." I don't think that's bad or good. That's what they used to call the people a long time ago who used to cross the river.

— *immigrant X in* Texas Monthly, *July 2006*

When I married a Texas Bubba, I learned some major life lessons—a pickup is a truck; a long neck is a beer; chili does not have beans; don't go dancing in sandals; na-a-sty has three syllables and so does Te-ex-as.

— *Sue Lorenz*

How true was the expression: "the windmill draws our water and the cows cut our wood." The lowly cowchips around which I at first tip-toed and raised my skirts held a place of high esteem.

—*Mary Blankenship*

20 Miles to Water
10 Miles to Wood
6 Inches to Hell
Gone Back East to Wife's Family
Make Yourself at Home
    —*scrawled on wall of abandoned West Texas pioneer dugout*

SOME OF THE FOLK SUPERSTITIONS STILL AROUND IN TEXAS INCLUDE THE FOLLOWING:

For the chills of malaria take a black string and tie a knot in it for every day you have had a chill; then add an extra knot for the current day, and hang the string in a dogwood tree. The chills will leave you.

Putting an axe under the bed will act as a contraceptive.

If the mesquite trees grow a big crop of beans, the coming year will be dry.

Sleep with a piece of wedding cake under your pillow, and you will dream of the one you will marry.

Sweep under a girl's feet, and she will not get married.

Make a wish before a falling star goes out of sight, and the wish will come true.

If you can keep from putting your tongue in the place from which a tooth is pulled, you will get some money or maybe a gold tooth.

If you're scared of lightning, twist the shoulder straps on your overalls, and lightning won't strike you.

If you dream of a wedding, you will hear of a death.

When someone in the family dies, the clock will stop.

When you hear three knocks on the door, you will hear of a death in the family.

If an owl perched on the roof top and hooted or screeched in the night, there would be a death in the family.

Texans traditionally eat black-eyed peas on New Year's Day for good luck.

East Texans depend on Mother Nature to give them signs to predict the weather. Some watch the habits of birds and animals:

- The chattering of flying squirrels in midwinter indicates an early spring.

- Severe weather can be expected when migrating birds wing south early.

- If the cat basks in February sun, it will warm itself by the stove in March.

- The early arrival of cranes in the fall indicates a cold winter.

- When squirrels are seldom seen in the fall, a cold winter is anticipated.

- When summer birds fly away, summer goes, too.

- If crows wing south, a cold winter will follow; if they fly north, the opposite is true.

—Tumbleweed Smith

We threw orange-colored love vine over a shoulder backward and
if it grew felt secure in our fancy's love.

—*Bertha McKee Dobie*

If a girl's second toe is longer than her big toe, she will rule
the house.

—*collected by Tressa Turner, folklorist*

A whistling girl and a crowing hen will come to no good end.

—*anonymous*

Cold hands, warm heart.

—*anonymous*

No one ever leaves Texas after they have been here a certain length of time. They either can't or don't want to, or it may be as the old settlers used to say, "having once drunk Red River water, it was not possible to go back . . ."

—*H. H. McConnell*

Keep Austin Weird.

—*unofficial mantra of the city of Austin*

X

ENGLISH IS GOOD ENOUGH FOR ME

Memorable Lines from Famous Texans

If English was good enough for Jesus Christ, it's good enough for me.

—*Miriam A. (Ma) Ferguson*

Never say die, say damn.

—*James Edward (Pa) Ferguson*

Never commit yourself until you are absolutely sure of your position, and once you give your word, keep it, even if it hurts.

—*Sam Rayburn*

Begin your day with labor and end it with laughter.

—Henri Castro

Do all you can, then do a little more. That's all there is to it.

—Bum Phillips

I try not to get frustrated over things I don't have much to do with.

—Tom Landry

Work is more fun than fun.

—Trammel Crow

You win by losing, hold on by letting go, increase by diminishing and multiply by dividing.

—Billie Sol Estes

Lessons are not to take the place of practice but to make practice worthwhile.

—Harvey Penick

You can talk to a fade, but a hook won't listen.

—Lee Trevino

Bravery is just determination to do a job that you know has
to be done.

—*Audie Murphy*

I never intended to become a run-of-the-mill person.

—*Barbara Jordan*

Two kinds of football players ain't worth a damn. One that never
does what he's told and the other that never does anything except
what he's told.

—*Bum Phillips*

Punt returns will kill you before a minnow can swim a dipper.

—*Darrell Royal*

People who know how much they're worth aren't usually worth that much.

—*Nelson Bunker Hunt*

There's a lot of uncertainty that's not clear in my mind.

—*Gibb Lewis*

Marriage isn't a word . . . it's a sentence!

—*King Vidor*

All I know about [big hair] is that my hairdresser says that women have big hair to balance a big behind.

—Ann Richards

There's as much risk in doing nothing as in doing something.

—Trammel Crow

Controversy, like beauty, is frequently in the eye of the beholder.

—Lyndon Baines Johnson

We like this kind of music [rock]. Jazz is strictly for the stay-at-homes.

—Buddy Holly

Hyperbole was to LBJ what oxygen is to life.

—Bill Moyers

Gentlemen, nothing funny ever happens on a football field.

—Tom Landry

There are two types of coaches. Them that have just been fired and them that are going to be fired.

—Bum Phillips

I wish I could find words to express the trueness, the loyalty to their trust and to each other of the old trail hands. I wish I could convey in language the feelings of companionship we had for one another.

—*Charles Goodnight*

To be successful as a team, you must bring all the parts together and play as one heartbeat.

—*Mack Brown*

Call me old-fashioned or starchy or whatever you will, but two things in this world I just can't grow accustomed to are a man and a woman living together without being married—and taking a mulligan at golf.

—*Harvey Penick*

A man who doesn't admire a good steer, a good horse, and a pretty woman, well, something is wrong with that man's head.

—*W. T. Waggoner*

Ninety-nine percent of the world's lovers are not with their first choice. That's what makes the jukebox play.

—*Willie Nelson*

All adventures, especially into new territory, are scary.

—*Sally K. Ride*

What convinces is conviction.

—*Lyndon Baines Johnson*

A little stress and adventure is good for you, if nothing else, just to prove you are alive.

—*Lady Bird Johnson*

If you're going to play the game properly you'd better know every rule.

—*Barbara Jordan*

I can go on and on talking about the grip until it gets too deep for me to understand.

—*Harvey Penick*

My mother's best advice was to always be able to look at myself in the mirror with no regrets. Like a fine racehorse, never quit until you cross the finish line.

—*Electra Waggoner Biggs*

I was nearly fifty when I began hiking, and later, backpacking, and whenever I would get to the top of something I thought I couldn't climb, I'd swell with pride and ask myself what other hills in my life might I now take on?

—*Linda Ellerbee*

I'd hate to have a guy who had to have a pep talk to get him to play.

—*Bum Phillips*

It's kind of like buying oats. If you want fresh oats, you got to buy fine-quality oats. But you can buy cheaper oats. The only problem is they've already been through the horse.

—*Gibb Lewis*

Any jackass can kick a barn down, but it takes a carpenter to build it.

—*Sam Rayburn*

I am not a paranoid deranged millionaire. Goddamit, I'm a billionaire.

—*Howard Hughes*

Money is like manure. Pile it all in one place and it stinks like hell. Spread it around and it does a lot of good.

—*Clint Murchison, Sr.*

I thrive on buying and selling. I just love making deals. It is like sports. It makes the adrenaline flow. Everything is out there for people to see.

—*Red McCombs*

To catch a mouse you've got to make noise like a cheese.

—*Charles Tandy*

They say familiarity breeds contempt. I don't believe that. I know my mother better than anyone and I don't have contempt for her.

—*Bum Phillips*

Some men "ripen" earlier than others and "burn out" early. Powder will flash but it won't last long.

—*Sam Rayburn*

Politics is a lot like football. You have to be smart enough to play the game and dumb enough to think it's important.

—*Ann Richards*

I've always felt that three things can happen to you whenever you throw the football, and two of them are bad.

—*Darrell Royal*

We don't care how they vote as long as we get to count them.

—*Lyndon Baines Johnson*

Every politician should have been born an orphan and remain
a bachelor.

—*Lady Bird Johnson*

Pickup trucks is one of the five things I know something about.
That and cold beer, BBQ'd ribs, gumbo, and chewing tobacco.

—*Bum Phillips*

Today our problem is not making miracles—but managing them.

—*Lyndon Baines Johnson*

You can't win them all—but you can try.

—*Mildred Ella (Babe) Didrikson Zaharias*

The clash of ideas is the sound of freedom.

—*Lady Bird Johnson*

Do not call for black power or green power. Call for brain power.

—*Barbara Jordan*

I know the law . . . I am its greatest transgressor.

—*Roy Bean*

There is no laughter in losing.

—Darrell Royal

If losing ever stops bothering you, it is time to do something else.

—Mack Brown

Nothing is more important in the face of war than cutting taxes.

—Tom DeLay

Having a lot of horse sense doesn't keep a man from acting
like a jackass.

—Sam Rayburn

The thing that decides the size of your funeral is the weather.

—*Bum Phillips*

Politics is the art of the possible.

—*Lyndon Baines Johnson*

In short, if you are not willing to be quoted by name, you should not be speaking.

—*John Connally*

Always be yourself. Don't try to be nobody else. If you do you'll make a fool of yourself and everybody will know it but you.

—*Tex Owens*

As coaches and parents, we can only teach our kids that life is a series of options, just like football. If you make good decisions, you are likely to succeed.

—*Mack Brown*

I would give out, just like a horse, and lay down in the road and drop off to sleep and when I would awaken the wolves would be all around me, snapping and snarling.

—*Charles Goodnight*

Dance is for everybody. I believe that the dance came from the people and that it should always be delivered back to the people.

—*Alvin Ailey*

In life, quality is what counts, not quantity.

—*Audie Murphy*

Perhaps no place in any community is so totally democratic as the town library. The only entrance requirement is interest.

—*Lady Bird Johnson*

It's an honor to be the first woman on the Supreme Court, but it will be even better when we get the second cowgirl on the Supreme Court.

—*Sandra Day O'Connor*

When I was a kid, our land was so poor we had to fertilize the house to raise the windows.

—Bum Phillips

∽

When anyone says he's a country boy, you better put your hand on your wallet.

—Lyndon Baines Johnson

∽

You cannot lead people by trying to drive them. Persuasion and reason are the only ways to lead them.

—Sam Rayburn

∽

Be positive in everything you do. Don't talk about the negatives. You can eat your life up being negative. The old statement about the glass being half-full or half-empty has merit, as far as I am concerned.

—*Mack Brown*

I can't make-believe worth a zinc cent.

—*Audie Murphy*

My doctor tells me I should start slowing it down—but there are more old drunks than there are old doctors so let's all have another round.

—*Willie Nelson*

I think I was singing when I was born.

—*Bob Wills*

No man that's in the wrong can stand up against a fellow that's in the right and keeps a-comin'.

—*Bill McDonald*

A long time ago down in Texas I learned that telling a man to go to hell and making him go there are two different propositions.

—*Lyndon Baines Johnson*

Friendship is nothing you can take from a guy. He's got to give it.

—*Bum Phillips*

What matters is not necessarily the size of the dog in the fight, it's the size of the fight in the dog.

—*Dwight David Eisenhower*

I am trying to show the world that we are all human beings and that color is not important. What is important is the quality of our work.

—*Alvin Ailey*

A politician's got to have publicity to live, but he can damn well get too much of it.

—*Sam Rayburn*

The First Lady is an unpaid public servant elected by one person— her husband.

—*Lady Bird Johnson*

I like the Army fine so far; they let you sleep in till 5:30. On the farm I had to get up at 4:00.

—*Audie Murphy*

Right now we're in the middle of a cultural war between the Muslims and the Western world. The politicians get in the way, but if you put two people together in a room, they can talk it out and work it out, just like Anna and the King.

—*Sandy Duncan*

Be sure you're right; then go ahead!

—*David Crockett*

A team that has character doesn't need stimulation.

—*Tom Landry*

The imperative is to define what is right and do it.

—*Barbara Jordan*

∿

It is easy to be an obstructionist; it's hard to be a constructionist.

—*Sam Rayburn*

∿

Big things that are distant too often take precedence over important things right under the nose.

—*Roy Bedichek*

∿

Thermopylae had her Messenger of Defeat, but the Alamo had none!
> —*attributed to Edward Burleson but*
> *likely furnished to him in a speech*

God made men stronger but not necessarily more intelligent.
He gave women intuition and femininity. And used properly, that
combination easily jumbles the brain of any man I've ever met.
> —*Farrah Fawcett*

The power I exert on the court depends on the power of my
arguments, not on my gender.
> —*Sandra Day O'Connor*

If you think you can, you're right; and if you think you can't,
you're right.

—*Mary Kay Ash*

It's not just enough to swing at the ball. You've got to loosen your
girdle and let 'er fly.

—*Mildred Ella (Babe) Didrikson Zaharias*

What difference does the uniform make? You don't hit with it.

—*Yogi Berra*

The older I get, the better I used to be.

—*Lee Trevino*

We got all the breaks and they were all bad.

—*Jimmy Phelan*

It is true that golf is a game in which you seem to get in touch with higher parts of yourself. We can say golf is spiritual in that respect. But we can't leave the body out of the golf swing, can we?

—*Harvey Penick*

Poverty dogged our every step. As soon as we grew old enough
to handle a plow, an ax or a hoe, we were thrown into the struggle
for existence.

—Audie Murphy

It's no disgrace to get knocked down as long as you get back up.

—Darrell Royal

It's good to have your eyes on the mountaintop, but as you're going
up that mountain, watch where you're walking.

—Mack Brown

Aerodynamically the bumblebee shouldn't be able to fly, but the bumblebee doesn't know that so it goes on flying anyway.

—*Mary Kay Ash*

Ya' gotta dance with who brung ya.

—*Darrell Royal*

You could make more money investing in government bonds, but football is more fun.

—*Clint Murchison, Jr.*

You never know when you'll be surrounded by Redskins.

—Tom Landry

When you pay someone to do something and he's doing it for the money, he'll do it but he really doesn't want to and he won't do it well. If he does it because he wants to do it and not because of money, he'll do a much better job.

—Jimmy Johnson

Par is whatever I say it is. I've got one hole that's a par 23 and yesterday I damn near birdied the sucker.

—Willie Nelson

I have played a lot of golf with preachers. One minister I recall would, after missing a short putt, turn to another member of the group and ask, "Would you mind expressing aloud my sentiments about that?"

—*Harvey Penick*

When I'm on a course and it starts to rain and lightning, I hold up my one iron cause I know even God can't hit a one iron.

—*Lee Trevino*

War robs you mentally and physically; it drains you. Things don't thrill you anymore. It's a struggle every day to find something interesting to do. It made me grow up too fast. You live so much on nervous excitement that when it is over, you fall apart.

—*Audie Murphy*

Uncommon Valor was a Common Virtue.

—Chester Nimitz

If a player is the least bit confused, he can't be aggressive. Tattoo that on your wall. Or better still, on your wallet. You must play aggressive football to win, and you cannot be aggressive and confused at the same time.

—Darrell Royal

The reason great teams win all the time is that they believe they can win all the time.

—Mack Brown

You must first know offense before you can coach defense.

—Tom Landry

Women make a difference in the public arena. Women look out for the needs of women and children, the elderly and the poor.

—Kathy Whitmire

As a woman, I have the right, no less than a man, to say and to prove that I value the reasons for living above mere life.

—Grace Halsell

I'd like to live long enough to see people not be surprised by the fact that a woman succeeded in something.

—*Oveta Culp Hobby*

Everyone wants to know they have made a difference, . . . I know I have. I may be tired, but I am not bored.

—*Sarah Weddington*

I am Woman—hear me roar. . . . Or is that my vacuum cleaner?

—*Liz Carpenter*

Sometimes when you get in a fight with a skunk, you can't tell who started it.

—*Lloyd Doggett*

Nothing is ever so bad that it can't be worse. Or better.

—*Bill Clements*

If you want to get along, go along.

—*Sam Rayburn*

You never lose a game if your opponent doesn't score.

—*Darrell Royal*

Athletes . . . who have had success in other sports, need to be humbled before they can learn the game of golf.

—*Harvey Penick*

There is no way to put a value on what high school coaches do for kids or on how hard their job is. They are, like other teachers, vastly underpaid, but very important to the future of our society.

—*Mack Brown*

There's nothing in the middle of the road but a yellow stripe and dead armadillos.

—*Jim Hightower*

The Congress will push me to raise taxes, and I'll say no, and they'll push, and I'll say no, and they'll push again. And all I can say to them is read my lips: No New Taxes.

—*George H. W. Bush*

I think that people want peace so much that one of these days government had better got out of their way and let them have it.

—*Dwight David Eisenhower*

I felt red, white and blue all over.

—*Ed White, as first American astronaut to walk in space*

You'll never get the full enjoyment out of this game hitting a slice. The only thing that can happen to a slice is, it will get worse.

—Harvey Penick

The only group in America that deserves to scrutinize what we are doing . . . are parents.

—Jack Valenti

I was already nine years old when I was born.

—Lee Trevino

I think I've figured out that there aren't very many ways to leave a [coaching] job and have people happy with you. The only way to leave a job and have people happy may be to die, and if you've been winning, then they may name something after you.

—*Mack Brown*

I miss the movies. Still, I understood that my kind of movie has had its day. I thought it was over for me.

—*Debbie Reynolds*

When I'm dead twenty-five years, people are going to begin to recognize me.

—*Scott Joplin*

Age may well bring dry rot as well as wisdom.

—*Sam Rayburn*

[N]othing is more important psychologically than knocking putts into the hole. Sinking putts makes your confidence soar, and it devastates your opponent.

—*Harvey Penick*

A president's hardest task is not to do what is right, but to know what's right.

—*Lyndon Baines Johnson*

If you've got it, you'll make it. If you don't have it, you won't.

—*Darrell Royal*

Do your own thing and build on what you can do, not on what somebody else didn't do.

—*Mack Brown*

It's the way you ride the trail that counts.

—*Dale Evans*

SELECTED BIBLIOGRAPHY

Armstrong, Lance. Every Second Counts. New York: Random House, 2003.

Banks, C. Stanley and Grace Taylor McMillan, eds. The Texas Reader: An Anthology of Romantic History, Biography, Legends, Folklore and Epic Stories of the Lone Star State. San Antonio: Naylor, 1947.

Carroll, Jeff. Being Texan: Celebrating a State of Mind. Bloomington: Authorhouse, 2004.

Chariton, Wallace O. Texas Wit & Wisdom. Plano: Wordware, 1990.

Cox, Mike. Texas Ranger Tales: Stories That Need Telling. Plano: Republic of Texas, 1997.

Crume, Paul. A Texan at Bay. New York: McGraw-Hill, 1961.

Dobie, J. Frank. The Flavor of Texas. Austin: Jenkins, 1975.

Faulk, John Henry. The Uncensored John Henry Faulk. Austin: Texas Monthly Press, 1985.

Flatau, Susie and Lou Halsell Rodenberger. Quotable Texas Women. Abilene: State House, 2005.

Growing Up in Texas. Austin: Encino, 1972.

Hale, Leon, Home Spun: A Collection. Houston: Winedale, 1997.

———. Turn South at the Second Bridge. Garden City, NY: Doubleday, 1965.

House, Boyce. *I Give You Texas!* San Antonio: Naylor, 1943.

Jent, Steven A. *A Browser's Book of Texas Quotations.* Plano: Republic of Texas, 2001.

Kent, Rosemary. *Texas Handbook.* New York: Workman, 1981.

Lich, Lera Patrick Tyler. *Larry McMurtry's Texas: Evolution of the Myth.* Austin: Eakin, 1987.

Maguire, Jack. *Talk of Texas.* Austin: Shoal Creek, 1973.

Minutaglio, Bill. *First Son: George W. Bush and the Bush Family Dynasty.* New York: Random House, 1999.

Penick, Harvey. *And If You Play Golf, You're My Friend: Further Reflections of a Grown Caddie.* New York: Simon & Schuster, 1993.

———. *Harvey Penick's Little Red Book: Lessons and Teachings from a Lifetime in Golf.* New York: Simon & Schuster, 1992.

Perry, George Sessions. *Texas: A World in Itself.* New York: Grosset & Dunlap, [1942] 1952

Phillips, Bob. *Texas Country Reporter: Stories from the Backroads.* Guilford, CT: Globe Pequot, 2000.

Pierce, PJ. *Let Me Tell You What I've Learned.* Austin: University of Texas Press, 2002.

Proulx, Annie. *That Old Ace in the Hole.* New York: Scribner, 2002.

Sellars, David K. *Texas Tales.* Dallas: Noble, 1955.

Shiffrin, Gale Hamilton. *Echoes from Women of the Alamo.* San Antonio: AW Press, 1999.

Smith, Tumbleweed. *Under the Chinaberry Tree.* Austin: Eakin, 2002.

Smithwick, Noah. *The Evolution of a State: or Recollections of Old Texas Days.* Austin: U of Texas P, [1900] 1983.

INDEX